THE DEE BRESTIN
BIBLE STUDY SERIES

A WOMAN OF
HEALTHY
Relationships

Building the New Generation of Believers

COOK COMMUNICATIONS MINISTRIES
Colorado Springs, Colorado • Paris, Ontario
KINGSWAY COMMUNICATIONS LTD
Eastbourne, England

The Dee Brestin Series
From Cook Communications Ministries
BOOKS

The Friendships of Women   We Are Sisters

The Friendships of Women Devotional Journal   We Are Sisters Devotional Journal

BIBLE STUDY GUIDES

A WOMAN OF LOVE
Using Our Gift for Intimacy (Ruth)

A WOMAN OF FAITH
Overcoming the World's Influences (Esther)

A WOMAN OF CONFIDENCE
Triumphing over Life's Trials (1 Peter)

A WOMAN OF PURPOSE
Walking with Jesus (Luke)

A WOMAN OF WORSHIP
Praying with Power (10 Psalms with a music CD)

A WOMAN OF HOSPITALITY
Loving the Biblical Approach (Topical)

A WOMAN OF MODERATION
Breaking the Chains of Poor Eating Habits (Topical)

A WOMAN OF CONTENTMENT
Insight into Life's Sorrows (Ecclesiastes)

A WOMAN OF BEAUTY
Becoming More Like Jesus (1, 2, 3 John)

A WOMAN OF PURPOSE

A WOMAN OF WISDOM
God's Practical Advice for Living (Proverbs)

A WOMAN OF HEALTHY RELATIONSHIPS
Sisters, Mothers, Daughters, Friends (Topical)

**THE FRIENDSHIPS OF WOMEN BIBLE
STUDY GUIDE correlates with
THE FRIENDSHIPS OF WOMEN**

NexGen® is an imprint of
Cook Communications Ministries, Colorado Springs, CO 80918
Cook Communications, Paris, Ontario
Kingsway Communications, Eastbourne, England

A WOMAN OF HEALTHY RELATIONSHIPS
© 2007 by Dee Brestin

Cover Design: Greg Jackson, Thinkpen Design, LLC.

First Printing, 2007
Printed in the United States of America
1 2 3 4 5 6 7 8 9 10

ISBN 978-0-7814-4446-0   060107

Contents

To My Daughter, Sally Brestin Hale

You are a woman, wife, and counselor now, and God has answered my prayers above and beyond what I asked. I asked Him to unleash your gift for intimacy—and He certainly has. The enormous suffering you have experienced in your young life has not been wasted, for you have pressed into God. You are a reflection of your father and your Father, loving others wisely and winsomely.

How I Thank God For:

The Team at Cook Communications Ministries: They've worked in harmony with their varied and amazing gifts to please the Lord. A special thanks to Karen Pickering, Janet Lee, Leigh Davidson, and Kerry Park. I would also wish to honor my late husband, who prayed continually for my quickening and supported my ministry, even when he was suffering so with his cancer. I believe he is still praying.

Introduction

"How good and how pleasant," Psalm 133 says, "when brethren dwell together in unity." God longs for families and the family of God to love well. Loving relationships don't just happen, for within each of us is a sin nature that works at cross-purposes with health and harmony. But it is possible, in Christ, to overcome our depravity and experience the sweetness God intended. As I look back over my relationships, I see, again and again, how He accomplished what I could not in my own strength.

* My marriage was going in a downward spiral because I thought that Steve was supposed to meet all my needs. But the Spirit awakened me that only God could do that, and He matured me to think not only of my own needs, but of Steve's. We were blessed, before the Lord took him home at the age of fifty-nine, with a marriage that was rare in its love and support.

* I had a tendency to cling too tightly to my women friends, again, looking to them for what only God could give me. The Lord showed me the difference between cherishing my friends and making them objects of worship. My friendships began to be transformed—moving from relational idolatry to helping one another find strength in God. My friendships are rich, rewarding, and soul-strengthening.

* I was a terrible mother, being ignorant of the scriptural principles of discipline. I tried to ignore the bad and reward the good and our firstborn toddler was in control of our home. The Lord opened my eyes through the book of Proverbs, transforming me as a mother. Today my five grown children are walking with the Lord.

* I stuck my foot in my mouth the first time I was a mother-in-law, but learned how to do the U-turn in repentance, and my daughter-in-law gave me grace. She is like a daughter now, loved dearly, and we experience such sweetness when we are together.

* When my mother lost her husband, health, and home, the Lord stressed to me the importance of being there for her. Through the Lord's mercy I was able to do that, even being there when she passed into glory. What sweet memories I cherish.

There is so much more. We will look at principles that affect all of our relationships. For those who want to go deeper with specific relationships, I would suggest the following guides.

The Friendships of Women (book and Bible study by that name—Life Journey, Cook Communications)

Building Your House on the Lord (marriage and parenthood—WaterBrook)

A Woman of Confidence (unbelieving husbands—NexGen, Cook Communications)

Falling in Love with Jesus, Living in Love with Jesus, Forever in Love with Jesus (Thomas Nelson)

Special Instructions for Preparation and Discussion

Just as good physical health takes work, so do healthy relationships. In this study:

1. Do your homework! Each day, same time, same place, to establish a habit. Each day, ask God to speak to you through His Word. Jesus says that "out of the overflow of our hearts" we speak. If you come to the study overflowing with insights, you will fill your sisters' cups.

2. In the discussion, be sensitive. The naturally talkative women need to exercise control and the shy women need to exercise courage to speak up.

3. Stay on target in the discussions. These lessons can be discussed in ninety minutes. If you don't have that much time, you have two options:

   A. Divide the lessons and meet for eighteen weeks. Do that week's prayer exercise both weeks.

   B. Do the whole lesson but discuss half the questions.

4. Follow the instructions for group prayer at the close of each lesson. Keep confidences in the group. There is power when we pray together.

One

The Vertical Relationship

I was devastated. My dearest friend and I had had a fight. We had discussed the "right" way to raise children. Shelly accused me of being too permissive. "Don't you know boundaries are important, Dee?"

Anger rose up in me and I flew back: "Of course I do! But you have so many boundaries I'm afraid your girls are going to rebel!"

We parted in tears.

I went to my husband, hoping for a little sympathy. Instead, Steve said, "Honey—I have heard you say, 'If there is a problem in a horizontal relationship, there is almost always a problem in your vertical relationship with the Lord.'"

Steve was speaking the truth to me, but often the truth is painful. Quite honestly, I'm not sure I would have had humility to respond rightly had God not had my attention in another way. I was right in the middle of writing my original edition of *The Friendships of Women*. I feared God enough to know that if I didn't walk the talk, He might not bless the book. So, I got alone with the Lord.

When I did that, He humbled me. Hadn't He shown me enormous grace? Hadn't He taught me that I should only speak the truth in love? Then, I repented. I wrote a note to Shelly with an apology. I also gave her a list of reasons why I loved her. A few days later I baked blueberry muffins and went to her home. When she opened the door, we fell into each other's arms weeping. She said, "I was going to forgive you, Dee—just not quite so quickly."

Then our tears turned to laughter as we both acknowledged our depravity. God not only restored our friendship, but has shown us, over the last twenty years, that I was too permissive as a mother and Shelly was too strict—and our friendship brought balance to our mothering!

11

Time and time again I've seen it happen: whether it is your relationship with your husband, friend, sister, or mother—when you get right with God, then you find yourself getting right with people.

Memory Work

In this study you will be memorizing the powerful closing of Romans 12: thirteen verses that will strengthen you for healthy relationships. Memorizing a passage rather than assorted verses increases retention. Memorizing one word at a time also increases retention. This week you will begin with the first verse.

> *Love must be sincere. Hate what is evil; cling to what is good.*
> Romans 12:9

WARMUP

Share your name with the group and also what you hope to see happen as a result of doing this study and being with these women.

DAY I
Salvation Is an Event

As a young wife and mother, I was angry with my husband. One night I said to him, in anger, "You are not meeting my needs!"

Gently, he said, "Honey—what are your needs?"

Not so gently, I cried, "You should be able to figure that out!"

I was under the false impression that a person, especially my husband, could meet my deepest needs. What I didn't realize is that only God could meet my deepest needs. The book of Ecclesiastes says:

> *He has made everything beautiful in its time. He has also set eternity in the hearts*
> *of men; yet they cannot fathom what God has done from beginning to end.*
> Ecclesiastes 3:11

God had been wooing me from the time I was a little girl, but I didn't come to my senses and accept Him as my savior until shortly after I had the above conversation with my husband. It was a few weeks later that my sister came and visited us. She had recently come to put her trust in Christ, and her life had been radically changed. That memorable weekend, she followed me around the apartment with a Bible, talking about Jesus. A month after she left, after reading the New Testament and crying out to God, I answered God's call and knelt in my bedroom to put my trust in the shed blood of Christ. God forgave me and saved me from His holy wrath. His Spirit came to live in me, giving me the new birth. My relationship with my husband—and with my toddler—dramatically changed. I began to see that much of the tension in our marriage was due to my unfair demands. God gave me a perspective and a purpose I had not had before. Our marriage began to improve.

Salvation is an event—but it is also a process. We are saved immediately from the wrath of God, but the refining process of changing bad habits to holy habits takes time. Salvation is also a process. But today, let's consider the event—for we must start there.

In your individual time with the Lord, begin the memory passage. Begin and end with the reference, and take it a word at a time. For example:

Romans 12:9

Love

Love must

Love must be …

1. Read Ephesians 1:3–4. According to verse 4, when did Jesus choose those who become believers?

> *He chose us in Him Before the creation of the world*

Salvation begins with God. He woos us. It may feel like we've taken the initiative, but if we look back over our lives, we can see His hand. Lauren Winner writes: "Sometimes, as in a great novel, you cannot see until you get to the end that God was leaving clues for you all along. Sometimes you wonder, "How did I miss it? Surely any idiot should have been able to see from the second chapter that it was Miss Scarlet in the conservatory with the rope" (*girl Meets God*, Algonquin, 2002, 57).

2. If you have put your trust in the shed blood of Christ, as you look back over your life before that moment, what "clues" can you see that God was wooing you?

> *- seeing His protection in my life*
> *- seeing His heart through prayer…*

If you have not yet put your trust in Christ, but are doing this Bible study, that is strong evidence that He is wooing you—and you can be so thankful.

3. According to Ephesians 1:4–5, what is God's purpose for salvation? How might this purpose affect our horizontal relationships?

> *To be holy & blameless in his sight… he predestined us to be adopted as his sons through Jesus — w/ His pleasure & His will!!*

13

4. According to Ephesians 1:7, how was our forgiveness made possible?

In Him we have redemption through His blood — forgiveness of our sins

5. According to Ephesians 2:8–10:

    A. By what are we not saved, and why, according to verse 9?

    * B. Whose workmanship are we and for what are we created, according to verse 10?

6. If you have put your trust in Christ, share, in one sentence, how you came to understand that salvation was through trusting the blood of Christ. (Hear from a few.)

7. Read Luke 19:1–9.

    A. How did Jesus woo Zacchaeus? (v. 5)

    B. How did Zacchaeus initially respond? (v. 6)

    C. What was the reputation of Zacchaeus? (v. 7)

D. What evidence do you see of sincere love and repentance in Zacchaeus? (v. 8) What does Jesus say concerning his salvation? (v. 9) How do you think some of Zacchaeus' relationships were immediately impacted?

8. Could you identify with either of Dee's relationship stories—either the one with her friend Shelly or the one with her husband? If so, how? Do you have a story on how Christ brought peace in a relationship? If so, share it briefly. (Hear from a few.)

DAY 2
Salvation Is Also a Process

When we receive Christ, we are given a new nature. A brand new baby is born, and that is definitely an event! When Zacchaeus repented, Jesus said, "Today, salvation has come to this house" (Luke 19:9a).

Yet salvation in its fullness is also a process. We are told, "Work out your salvation with fear and trembling, for it is God who works in you to will and to act according to his good purpose" (Philippians 2:12–13). The day I put my trust in Christ I was born again, and I was definitely changed. But, oh, I had (and have, even forty years later) so far to go. Salvation is also a process, for it takes time to be conformed to the image of Christ. Today we'll begin to consider what it means "to work out our salvation." For as we mature in our salvation, our relationships are transformed.

Memory Work

Continue your Memory Work.

Scripture Study

9. Read Hebrews 10:14. Find a phrase describing the event of salvation in the first part of this verse and then a phrase describing the process of salvation in the latter part of the verse.

10. Read Philippians 2:12–13 again.

   A. The Philippians have been obedient when Paul is present—what other time, according to verse 12, does he want them to be obedient?

   B. When we are obedient only when others are watching, what does that indicate?

   C. What are they to work out according to verse 12?

This is the fullness of salvation, the sanctifying process that occurs through the power of God. As we die to ourselves, His resurrection power increases. This is the process of sanctification, of becoming conformed to the image of Christ.

   D. According to verse 13, how do we know we are not working on our own?

11. Read Philippians 2:14–15.

   A. What command is given in verse 14?

   * B. What reason for the command is given in verse 15?

   C. How does this fit into "the process of salvation?"

D. How might you apply this today?

DAY 3
A New Commandment

One of the things I've learned both in Scripture and in life is that important things are said when time is running out. I was at the deathbed of my mother less than a year ago. My sister called from the airport. "Is she still alive?"

"Yes, Bonnie, she is. I think she's waiting for you."

When Bonnie arrived, she rushed to the bed, weeping. Mother opened her eyes and gave her a weak smile. Bonnie leaned down, her words overflowing from her heart: "Oh, Mother—I'm so thankful you are still here. I was in Nova Scotia. That means 'New Scotland' and so much reminded me of you. I understood your heritage better and what helped make you such a fun and creative mother! They danced in the city square, they sang, they told wonderful stories—I felt like I was with you! Oh, Mom—I'll love you forever."

Important things are said when time is running out. When time was running out for Jesus, He told His disciples that He would love them forever. He also gave them an important "new commandment," the passage you are memorizing this week and next.

Getting along with other believers isn't optional. It's commanded. Even though some of our brothers and sisters may be very difficult, Jesus commanded us to love them. As we obey, an amazing thing happens—the love of God actually grows in our hearts, helping us to become conformed to His image.

Memory Work

Continue your Memory Work of Romans 12:9.

Scripture Study

12. Skim John 13. What is the setting? How much time did Jesus have left before His death?

13. Read John 13:33–35.

    A. What three things does Jesus tell His disciples in verse 33?

    B. What feelings do you think they might have had upon hearing these three things?

    C. What kind of emotions do you have or might you have, when you know you are saying a very long good-bye to someone you love?

    D. Have you had the experience of hearing or saying important things "when time is running out?" If so, share briefly.

    E. What command does Jesus give in verse 34? How is this different from the command to love our neighbor?

    F. What does Jesus say will happen if we love one another? (v. 35)

    G. Did the love of believers for one another (or for you) play any part in your salvation (consider both the event and the process)? If so, share how briefly.

DAY 4
That We May Be One

Sandi and Marilyn were cochairs of women's ministries at a large city church. In-depth Bible studies were thriving, as well as ministries for young moms, singles, and the elderly. But then a rift between them changed everything. The fissure rippled out, dividing the women in the ministry, sapping energy and diminishing fruit. "Looking back fifteen years later," Sandi recalls, "I can't tell you how deeply I regret not humbling myself and reconciling with Marilyn sooner—before so much damage was done."

Satan wants to divide the sheep, because he knows that united we stand, divided we fall. He also knows how the world views division among us. They think, "Why would I want that?"

Jesus didn't just tell us to love one another, He supplied us with tools. Today we'll study a prayer Jesus prayed for us. In this prayer He mentions the tools by which we can overcome our flesh so that we might be one.

This prayer was prayed just before Jesus went to the cross. Again, remember, important things are said when time is running out.

Memory Work

Review your Memory Work.

Scripture Study

14. What is the bad news and the good news of John 16:33?

15. Read John 17:1–3.

    A. What time has come? (v. 1) What authority did God grant Jesus? (v. 2)

    B. What is eternal life? (v. 3)

16. Read John 17:13–19. Name three requests below that Jesus makes in this passage.

As you consider each of these three things, explain why each is supernatural rather than natural, and also, why it is needed for healthy relationships.

* A. Verse 13 (Why supernatural and why needed?)

* B. Verse 15 (Why supernatural and why needed?)

C. Verse 17 (Why supernatural and why needed?)

17. Read John 17:20–23.

A. Now, for whom does Jesus pray? (v. 20)

B. For what precisely does He pray and why? (v. 21)

C. How does the world respond when we, as believers, are one? When we are feuding?

D. When you have a disagreement with another believer, do you consider that Satan may be involved? Why might this be important?

18. Is there a relationship with another believer that is strained? Is there tension within your local church? If Satan is involved, he is breathing lies to you. Consider this, and ask yourself, "How might I use the Word of truth to defeat the Enemy in this case?"

DAY 5

As We Choose to Love, His Love Grows in Us

Did you know that the Bible teaches that as we love, His love becomes complete in us? Over and over again, John tells us,

> If we love one another, God lives in us and his love is made complete in us. (1 John 4:12)

This is how sanctification happens. This is how "working out" the fullness of salvation happens. We walk in the light, and His light grows stronger in us. We love, and His love is made complete in us. This is what this Bible study will explore in depth.

But in closing today, consider how you can love well within your small group. (Or, if you are doing this study alone, apply it to those close to you.) In small groups, you have all kinds of opportunities to choose to love. To keep this group healthy and flowing with love, consider how the following Scriptures could be applied.

Memory Work

Review your Memory Work.

Scripture Study

19. How might you love one another well in this group? Come up with at least three specific applications for how you might show love to this group.

20. What does Colossians 3:16 say? How might you apply this to showing love in this group?

21. How would loving one another apply to:

    A. Listening in the group? (What makes a good listener?)

    B. Being honest about your needs—are you willing to share where you are struggling with character issues instead of just asking for prayer for another's illness? (That is important too—but too often our prayer times dodge the central issue of our own sin and need for sanctification.)

    C. Keeping confidences?

    D. Showing you care about people outside of group time—what might this look like?

Prayer Time*

Break into groups of three or four. Have one woman share, in prayer, a way she would like to grow. Have the other women support her. Then the next woman should lift up her need. It might look something like this:

Patti: Please help me get into the habit of doing my homework.

Lorinda: Yes, Lord.

Trish: I agree, Lord.

Lorinda: Lord, please show me how to love my daughter well.

Patti: Please give Lorinda wisdom and love.

Trish: Yes, Lord.

Two

Never Underestimate the Power of a Mother

S tudies are clear: the role of the mother has an enormous impact on the ability of a child to love. If she is not present in the formative years, physically or emotionally, the negative effect on the child is dramatic. The Swiss physician Paul Tournier explains in *The Gift of Feeling* (John Knox Press, 1979) that it has been firmly established scientifically that the child needs his mother in the first year of life. "His mental health during the whole of the rest of his life can depend on it."

When my husband and I walked through the orphanage in Bang-Kok from which we adopted our daughter, the children rocked back and forth, stared into space, and were emotionally distant. What had been missing in their lives? A mother's love. They hadn't been held, hadn't been nurtured, and hadn't been loved. They picked on each other, increasing their trauma. For most, it seemed "too late." Our daughter Beth was one of the twelve of five-hundred children that the social workers called a "survivor." What had she survived? The lack of a mother's love.

If you were not loved well by your mother, there is still hope, for nothing is impossible with God. In the next chapter we'll consider those who didn't receive the blessing of a mother's love.

Let's begin in Exodus with some positive models of mother love. Whether or not you are a mother, this chapter is relevant, for there are so many "motherless" young women out there who need women to stand in the gap.

Memory Work

> *Be devoted to one another in brotherly love. Honor one another above yourselves. Never be lacking in zeal, but keep your spiritual fervor, serving the Lord.*
> Romans 12:10–11

WARMUP

Have each woman share, in a sentence, one way her mother showed her or taught her how to love. If she was not loved well, she could choose someone who was a positive mother-figure to her. (Give women the freedom to pass.)

DAY I

The Hebrew Midwives

They were told to kill the boy babies—and yet, they found a way to defy the king.

I've always been intrigued by the exhortation in 1 Peter to women. Here we are told that we can become like the holy women of old if we "do what is right and do not give way to fear" (1 Peter 3:6c). That's good advice for life, and good advice for motherhood.

The Hebrew midwives easily could have given way to fear. The king could have had them beheaded for their disobedience. But when you fear and love God, it helps you be an overcomer—no matter how great the pressure is.

This is relevant to us—for the pressures against being a good mother in our culture are enormous. It begins immediately, for oftentimes there may be pressure to end the life of your baby. If you are one of the many women who succumbed to the pressure, I realize these lessons may be painful, but also, they may be a door of hope for you.

Memory Work

Continue your Memory Work.

Scripture Study

1. Read Exodus 1:8–14.

   A. What was the king's concern and his plan to solve it? (vv. 8–10)

   B. What was Plan A? How did it backfire? (vv. 11–12)

2. Read Exodus 1:15–21.

A. What orders did the king himself give to Shiphrah and Puah? (vv. 15–16)

Not often are names of women recorded in Scripture. When they are, it is significant.

B. Consider the treachery of these orders. How would they have to deceive the women they were going to help? Who was to be the executioner?

C. Why didn't the midwives obey? (v. 17)

D. How did the midwives answer the king? (vv. 18–19)

E. How did God respond to the midwives? (vv. 20–21)

As you study the holocausts throughout history against the Jews, it is not hard to see the hand of Satan. Certainly, he wanted to avoid the birth of the Messiah. He has always been eager to cause God's people to despair and to curse God. His goal is not so much to make us miserable, but to make God look bad.

3. What does Satan do according to John 10:10?

4. The following are lies from the Enemy that women have believed that have led them

to end the life of their child. Counteract each lie with a truth from Scripture. (Some are given in parentheses, but you may think of others.)

A. You cannot afford a baby now. (Matthew 6:33)

B. God doesn't care about you. (Matthew 10:29)

C. You don't have the energy to take care of another baby now. (Matthew 11:28)

D. You don't want people to know you are pregnant. (Ecclesiastes 12:13–14)

E. You've done it before, why not do it again? (Hebrews 3:12–13; Proverbs 29:1)

F. It's legal—and a lot of people think it is right—so how it can be wrong? (Proverbs 14:12; Proverbs 11:21)

* G. Perhaps this baby can come back and be born another time—perhaps reincarnation is true. (Hebrews 9:27)

H. This isn't really a baby—just a blob of tissue. (Psalm 139:13–16)

Lee Ezell is a woman who chose to give her baby, conceived in rape, life. She also chose to place her with an adoptive family. This baby was the only baby she was ever able to have and is a daughter who is so like Lee. They are now close and the daughter speaks up for those babies who are conceived in rape. Lee said, reflectively, "I've learned that often the wrong decision seems easier at first, but leads to great pain later—and the right decision seems harder at first, but leads to great peace later." (*The Missing Piece*, Bantam Books, 1988)

DAY 2
If You (or Someone You Love) Have Aborted a Baby

The Hebrew midwives went down in history and were honored by God because they stood up to enormous pressure. They feared God and that fear kept them safe from the lies of the Enemy and the pressure of the Pharaoh.

But so many women are deceived by the lies of the Enemy and make a choice they regret for the rest of their lives. Forty-three percent of women today in America will have at least one abortion by the time they are forty-five. (*Facts in Brief*, Alan Guttmacher Institute: January, 1997). That includes many Christians as well. In fact, Christians may choose to abort to cover up sexual sin—but the reality is that though they might succeed in covering up sin from other people, they cannot hide from God or their own souls. As a result, an emotional and spiritual wound is created that if not attended to, will haunt them, one way or another, until they deal with the truth. Many never deal with their past actions and are haunted forever. One post-abortive woman tells her story, and urges women to seek out a post-abortion support group:

> I did everything I could to try to cover up what I'd done. My wound was festering and oozing, but I put a big bandage over it so I could pretend it wasn't there. But it continued to throb and fester, and the poison spread to my relationship with my husband, my living children, my friends, and my God. Every time someone mentioned the "A" word, I cringed in pain, especially in church.
>
> Though I confessed my sin to God, I felt like what I had done was unforgivable—so I continued in pain.
>
> What changed all that was being involved in a post-abortion support group at our local Pregnancy Resource Center. It was scary to go. Scary to admit what I'd done to others—but it's one of the best decisions I ever made. During the

Bible study we ripped off the bandages and exposed our wounds to God, to each other, and even to ourselves. Just as going to a doctor can be painful at first, so was this—but, oh, the relief when healing began! Facing the dark parts of my past in a safe, confidential, and nonjudgmental environment was the beginning. Just being in a room with women who really understood because they'd been there was so freeing. The isolation was finally broken. Hearing the truth of God through His Word, and of His power to make the darkest crimson stain as white as snow, brought me such peace. And when I allowed myself to grieve, not just for my sin, but for the loss of my children (for I had aborted twice), God brought a wholeness to my life I never had thought was possible. Truly, I am set free. Now I can be a healthy wife, mother, friend, and child of God.

5. Read Psalm 32.

   A. Write down everything you can discover about the person who is blessed from verses 1–2.

   B. Write down everything you can discover about the person who is silent about her sin from verses 3–4.

   C. What happens to the one who confesses her sin? (vv. 5–8)

   D. What must we not be like and why? (vv. 9–10)

6. Why does James 5:16 exhort us to confess our sins to one another?

DAY 3
• •
Jochebed: She Did What She Could

She was an amazing mother. Not only did she not give way to fear, she truly trusted God and saw Him come through for her in amazing ways. She makes it into the "Hebrews' Hall of Fame" for her courage and faith in mothering. She raised three amazing children. Moses and Aaron were used of God to bring His people out of slavery in Egypt. There were many times when they could have been overcome by fear—but I'm sure their mother's example strengthened them. Miriam became a leader of the Israelite women. Though all three of these individuals had their times of weakness, their lives counted for God.

Jochebed was not only a mother, but a mentor. Speaker Jennie Dimkoff imagined that Jochebed taught her daughter Miriam (who was probably between six and nine) crucial nurturing skills: how to keep a baby quiet when soldiers are prowling; how to keep a baby safe when his basket is floating in the crocodile-infested Nile; and how to respond convincingly if their prayers were answered and the princess found Moses.

Write out your Memory Work and then check it for errors.

7. What was the king's third plan to reduce the Israelites, according to Exodus 1:22?

8. How would you have felt if you became pregnant in times like these? Have you ever questioned the timing of a pregnancy in your life? Or His timing, in general? What truth would you breathe into your soul?

His timing, so often, is not ours, yet His timing is best. Matthew Henry writes,

> Observe the beauty of providence: just at the time when Pharaoh's cruelty rose to this height the deliverer was born ... (*Matthew Henry's Commentary*, Volume 1, New Modern Edition, Hendrickson, 2003, p. 217)

9. Enormous prayer and planning must have gone into Jochebed's attempt to save Moses. In a sense, she made an adoption plan by choosing what was best for her child. Read between the lines and describe what she might have had to pray and do in each of the following steps:

   A. Exodus 2:2 (Using your imagination, how might she have hidden him, kept him quiet?)

B. Exodus 2:3 (How did she waterproof it?)

C. Exodus 2:4 (Using your imagination, how might she have trained Miriam?)

10. What are some of the ways a mother could train her older children to care for the younger children? Be specific—and consider not just the early years, but elementary and teen years.

11. Write down everything you learn about Jochebed from Hebrews 11:23.

12. If you are a mother, what are some of the biggest spiritual and physical dangers that face your child or children? (This varies in different seasons of life—so consider where they are right now.) How might you be proactive against these dangers, as Jochebed was?

DAY 4
Jochebed: She Let the Basket Go

Mrs. Dimkoff imagines Jochebed's parting before she leaves her children at sunrise:

She holds Moses one last time, feeling the velvet softness of his face in her neck, and her heart hurts. She puts him in the basket and covers him carefully.

She hitches up her skirt in her waistband, picks up that basket on her hip, and steps into the reeds while Miriam, with pounding heart, watches. Then Jochebed comes back on shore and faces a little girl, saying: "Remember everything we practiced, Honey … I love you so—Oh, don't be afraid Miriam—God is with you." And then she does the hardest thing in her life. She walks away from her two vulnerable children and leaves them in God's hands.
("Choosing to Trust," JennieDimkoff.com)

13. Read Exodus 2:5–10.

A. What providences of God can you see in verses 5–6?

B. What does Miriam ask? Do you think this was preplanned with her mother? Why or why not?

C. What two providences of God can you see in verse 9?

D. What hard thing did Jochebed have to do again when Moses was older? (v. 10)

Jochebed no doubt nursed Moses for as long as she could! The bond that occurs for mothers who are nursing their babies is an especially strong one. Connie Marshner, author of *Can Motherhood Survive? A Christian Looks at Social Parenting* describes her relationship with her toddler:

By the time Caroline was a year-and-a-half old … we had an elaborate lovers' ritual to follow. When she was ready for bed, in double diapers and pajamas, I'd ask her, "Do you want some mama nursee?" She'd nod or say yes and start smiling with intense delight…. She'd climb up the steps by herself and then run, literally run, to the rocking chair in the corner of her room. She'd climb up on it and sit over to one side, looking at me with eager expectation, total attention, and that wonderful smile. Then I'd sit down, and she'd arrange herself in my lap. Within two minutes, total contentment would absorb her and those blue-gray eyes would close. Calling it a lovers' ritual is not an exaggeration: I was her first love, and the depth and completeness of my response to her taught her about the possibilities of love for the rest of her life. (Wolgemuth and Hyatt, 1990, p. 31)

14. Many mothers are discouraged from nursing their babies for a myriad of reasons—most of them cultural. If you nursed your children, what encouragement can you give to other young mothers to try to do so?

15. One of the hardest things we must do as mothers is to let go of our children. Can you share a time when your mother or you let go of a child, by faith, and saw God come through? If so, share briefly.

DAY 5

Faith and Mothering

One of the ways we experience the fullness of our salvation, our sanctification, is to walk by faith. When we take baby steps of faith, and see Him meet us, we are encouraged to step out again.

Surely one area where we are asked to exercise faith in mothering is in "letting the basket go." God's plan is that we do such a good job of training our children in the Lord when they are young that they become strong in Him, capable of flying free. When we hang on to our children, fearful of letting them try their wings, or fearful of letting them experience the consequences of their own bad choices, we cripple them. They stay close—but this is not a healthy mother/child relationship. This is what is called codependency—one is needed and the other needs to be needed. God's plan is for us to mature to depend on Him alone.

This doesn't mean that our children won't experience pain when they first fly out of the nest. Pain is one of the ways we grow. But God will be with them. He will be with them and show them how to recover from broken hearts and broken bank accounts. He will also be with them in danger. I remember when one of my daughters called because she was in an extremely dangerous situation overseas, and there was no way her dad or I could get to her quickly. In my prayer diary I wrote, "Oh, Lord—please send someone who can be the kindness of God to her, who can protect her and send her to safety." When this daughter was in the height of peril, a woman came to her aid, rescuing her, hiding her, and sending her home. Later I found out the woman's name meant, "the kindness of God."

Sometimes we simply cannot protect our children. They will experience pain. I wanted so to protect my children from losing their father. But Steve died of colon cancer. What has amazed me is to see how God has been a father to the fatherless, and how my children's souls have been enlarged by their suffering.

He is there, and He is not silent. He cares for our children even more than we do, and He calls us, sooner or later, "to let the basket go."

Memory Work

Review your Memory Work.

Scripture Study

16. Read Exodus 3:1–15.

    A. What calling did God have for the life of Moses? (v. 10)

    B. What was Moses' first response? (v. 11)

    C. What was God's reassuring answer? (v. 12)

    D. What was Moses' next question? (v. 13)

E. What was God's answer? (v. 14)

The name "I AM" is, literally, "I AM that I AM" (I AM twice). God is so "other" He can only be compared to Himself. This is the same name that Jesus uses in all the I AM's of John. (I AM the Light of the World; I AM the Vine; I AM the Good Shepherd ...) Not only did He promise to be with Moses, He has promised to be with each of us, as His children, as His sheep. Our children may face enormous challenges, but God will be with them.

17. If you are a mother, can you share a time when you saw God be with your child?

18. Have your parents been able to see that God is with you? If so, share one way.

19. Why is it important for us not to continually protect our children from the consequences of their choices? How is this part of "letting the basket" go?

20. What do you think you will remember from this lesson? How will you apply it?

Prayer Time

Break into groups of three or four. Each woman should take turns sharing her answer to the last question and then the others can support her. Then go around again, giving women the opportunity to share another request and receive support.

Three

Breaking the Chain in Christ

Lee Ezell was one of the authors asked by Gloria Gaither to contribute to her book, *What My Parents Did Right* (Star Song, 1991, pp. 217-220). Lee's story was in the final section of the book, entitled "You Can Break the Cycle." Here were stories of people who were raised in dysfunctional homes, yet had been set free through the grace of God to break the cycle of destructive habit patterns.

Lee's father was a violent alcoholic and her mother had retreated behind a "Great Emotional Wall" to protect herself. Unfortunately, that wall also shielded Lee's mother from her children. Lee says, "Mother was a veritable fortress. In my home, there was never any expression of caring or love; I knew only defensive survival tactics."

Yet, Lee is a miracle of a soul set free. As a young woman, Lee came to Christ through a Billy Graham Crusade. God also, in His grace, brought a godly older woman into her life who gave Lee the mothering, albeit late, that she had never known. Today, Lee is a caring mother and knows the joy of deep friendships with other women. Lee says, "I am through playing the Blame Game." Lee knows she will give an account of herself to God, and that she cannot blame her parents for her sin. (In Ezekiel 18:1–3, God told the Israelites the same thing—that they should no longer find refuge behind the sin of their parents!) We have the resources in Christ to break the chain of destructive habit patterns.

Memory Work

Be joyful in hope, patient in affliction, faithful in prayer.
Romans 12:12

WARMUP

Some of the ways for parents to give their children the blessing are the spoken or written word, gifts, acts of service, picturing a bright future, or physical touch. When recently have you been blessed in one of these ways and how?

DAY I
When Your Parents Can't Give You the Blessing

Jacob and Esau were victims of parental favoritism and suffered enormously. Esau articulates that pain when he discovers that his father has given his blessing to his brother, and cries, weeping: "Bless me—me too, my father!" (Genesis 27:34).

In their classic book, *The Blessing*, John Trent and Gary Smalley say that Esau's anguished cry is being echoed today by many: "Some will try to break down the door to their parents' hearts to receive this missed blessing, but all too often their attempt fails. For whatever reason, they have to face the fact that their blessing will have to come from another source" (Thomas Nelson, 1986, p. 17).

This week we'll begin with Hagar, the unloved concubine wife of Abraham. How did she become a slave? Was she torn from the arms of her parents? Examined on the auction block like an animal? Certainly she was treated like property. Hagar was utterly alone in the world. In one of Abram and Sarai's less shining moments, Hagar was going to be used and abused. Who would protect her? Who would give her the blessing?

Memory Work

Review your Memory Work of Romans 12:9–11.

Scripture Study

1. Read Genesis 16.

   A. List everything you learn about Hagar in the first three verses. What reasons can you see for pain in her life?

   B. According to verse 4, describe what happened to Hagar and how she responded to Sarai.

C. Though Hagar's attitude was wrong, why might we have empathy for her?

D. What does Sarai tell Abram in verse 5? How does she fail to take responsibility for her actions?

* E. How does Abram fail to protect Hagar in verse 6? Why do you think he shirked his responsibility?

F. What evidence can you find in verse 7 for God's seeking Hagar out?

G. In verse 8, what question is Hagar asked, and how does she respond?

I love to hear someone speak the truth, even when the consequences may be painful, because it shows they fear God more than men. Recently my eight-year-old grandson disobeyed his mother. His dad asked him if he forgot or if he disobeyed. Simeon thought for a long moment and then said, "I disobeyed."

H. What hard thing does the angel tell Hagar to do in verse 9?

I. After receiving the prophecy concerning her son, what does Hagar do in verse 13?

No one else in Scripture—male or female—ever names God. Hagar does. She names Him El Roi, "the God who sees me." The new name she gives to God expresses her most basic theological conviction. She is not invisible to God (Carolyn Custis James, *Lost Women of the Bible*, Zondervan, 2005, p. 95).

J. What is the place named? What does this mean? (vv. 13–14)

2. Share a time when you were very aware that the Lord saw you. (Keep it brief!)

DAY 2 ....

He Sees You and He Hears Your Cry

Abandoned as a baby, our daughter Beth spent her first twelve years in an orphanage in Thailand. Unloved and abused, she cried out to God. When my husband and I prayed about adopting another child, as we were silent before God, my husband heard a little girl crying.

A child that has no value in the eyes of the world is precious to God. I am absolutely convinced that God placed Beth in our family, for "God sets the lonely in families" (Psalm 68:6a).

When Isaac the child of promise was born, Sarah wanted Hagar and her son Ishmael cast out, and God told Abraham to listen to Sarah. Cast out into the desert, with nothing but a little food and a flask of water, Hagar was overcome by grief.

Again, God comes to her. No matter the pain in your life, God sees. He hears. He is close to the broken-hearted. Though you may not have been loved well by a husband, by a friend—or even by a father and mother, God always loves you. The psalmist says, "Though my father and mother forsake me, the Lord will receive me" (Psalm 27:10). God longs to give you the blessing.

Begin memorizing Romans 12:12.

3. Read Genesis 21:1–21.

A. What promise did the Lord keep to Sarah? (vv. 1–7)

B. What did Sarah ask of Abraham? (v. 10)

C. How did Abraham respond, and what did God tell him to do? (vv. 11–13)

D. Describe Hagar's situation in detail. (vv. 14–16) Imagine how you might feel in this situation.

E. Who heard the boy crying? What did the angel say? (vv. 17–18)

F. What did God do next? What is He communicating to her through this? (v. 19)

G. What do we learn in verse 20?

4. Read Psalm 139:1–16. Write down the phrases that are particularly meaningful to you and explain why they are meaningful.

5. What does the story of Hagar communicate to you? What relevance does this have for you today?

DAY 3
The Sins of the Fathers

There truly is such a thing as generational sin. The sins of the fathers (and the mothers) ripple out to the next generation, and the next, and the next.

The proverb "like mother, like daughter" is actually found in Ezekiel 16:44, and is used in a negative sense of God's people. Instead of acting like His children, they adopted the practices of their fathers and mothers, who had copied the practices of pagan nations—engaging in idolatry, prostitution, and child sacrifice. The church is impacted by the generation of believers that went before. As America has prospered, many believers have come to think they are entitled to a life that is relatively free of trouble—and are angry at God when trouble comes. Churches have become consumer-oriented, driven to meet "felt needs," instead of asking for people to die to themselves. We are often proud, greedy, and selfish. In the church we've often not taken the holiness of God seriously and have neither loved Him well nor one another well.

How interesting to see in the Scripture that confession of sin, not only personal sin, but the "sins of their fathers," often preceded revival. These confessing believers did not disassociate themselves from their fathers or the corporate body of believers, but numbered themselves with them, pleading for mercy.

The Israelites were in slavery as a result of the sins of their fathers. In a metaphorical way, the same can be true of us. The good news is that the chain of sin can be broken in Christ—but first, it must be recognized, confessed, and turned from.

Memory Work

Continue your Memory Work.

Praise

Spend some time in praise. Nehemiah sent out the choirs before the dedication of the wall (Nehemiah 12:31, 38). Praise defeats the Enemy!

Scripture Study

6. Read Leviticus 26:40–42. Find everything that God's people are exhorted to do in this passage in order for Him to "remember His covenant" with them.

7. How does the psalmist pray in Psalm 79:8?

8. Read Nehemiah 1:3–8.

    A. Why was Nehemiah grieved? What does this tell you about his heart?

    B. Whose sins did Nehemiah confess?

    * C. What reasons can you see for our confessing the sins of our fathers, of our nation, and of the body of Christ?

The books of Ezra and Nehemiah took place after Cyrus released the Jewish captives to go home to Jerusalem. During this time, under these godly leaders, there was revival and rebuilding of the temple in Jerusalem.

9. Read Nehemiah 8:1–10.

    A. What did Ezra do and what was the attitude of the people? (vv. 1–8)

   B. What did the governor, Nehemiah, tell them? (vv. 9–10)

10. Read Nehemiah 9:1–3.

   A. Describe what the Israelites did according to verse 1?

   B. What else did they do, according to verse 2?

   C. What, according to verse 3, did they do for a quarter of the day—and what did they do for another quarter of the day?

11. Read Nehemiah 9:4–38. What are some of the sins of the fathers that they confessed? What value do you see in their confession—for themselves and for future generations?

12. Following the model of Ezra and Nehemiah, write down some of the ways you can see that God's people in recent generations have been forgetting Him and His holiness. Then, number yourself with them and confess, privately to Him, their sin and yours, pleading for mercy.

DAY 4

God Calls Us to Break the Chain

Just as corporate sins affect God's people, so do the individual sins of our parents, grandparents, and great-grandparents affect us. Children of abuse are prone to become abusers, children of divorce are prone to divorce, children of alcoholics are prone to become alcoholics.... When I speak in the jails I am saddened to see so many mothers and daughters there together.

But there is great hope in Christ. My daughter-in-law looked back over her generations and said, "I don't know of any marriages in my family that stayed together—but it is stopping here, because of Jesus." She and my son have a strong marriage and are modeling that to their children. We don't have to perpetuate the sins of the past, though it is helpful to recognize what they were, for we are vulnerable to repeating them. We must be proactive about breaking the chain. That involves insight, prayer, seeking out positive role models, and often, professional Christian counseling. If your mother did not know how to mother well, seek out a godly mother and spend time with her. If your parents did not have a Christian home, seek out those who do, and spend time with them. If the sins of your parents led to great emotional scars, professional Christian counseling is vital.

During the rest of this week we'll look at a chain of sin and at the woman who, through the power of God, saw that chain broken. Today is vital background information, but be sure to get to the application tomorrow!

Memory Work

Write out Romans 12:9–12 from memory and check it for errors.

Scripture Study

13. What do you discover about the origin of the Moabites in Genesis 19:30–36? Summarize the sin of the daughters.

14. Describe the sin of the Moabite women in Numbers 25:1–3. How did the Israelites respond and how did God respond?

The gods of Moab, Baal and Chemosh, were thought to desire sexual immorality in the temple. The superstition held was that when these gods saw people having intercourse, they would be inspired to make their crops fertile.

15. Read Deuteronomy 23:3–6. What command does the Lord make about the Moabites (and Ammonites) and why?

"The tenth generation" is a way of saying "forever."

Moab was rich and fertile. It's one of the reasons Elimelech was tempted to take his wife Naomi and two sons there during the famine in Bethlehem. God had clearly told the Israelites not to intermarry with Moabite women (1 Kings 11:1–2).

16. Read the following verses from the prophet Isaiah and describe what he saw in the distant future concerning Moab:

A. Isaiah 15:1–5

B. Isaiah 16:2

C. Isaiah 16:6–7

D. Isaiah 16:11–14

Zephaniah 2:9 also says that Moab will be destroyed like Sodom and Gomorrah. All of these prophecies were fulfilled after the time of Ruth. Symbolically, Moab represents what can happen to any of us if we continue in the sins of our ancestors. Not only is misery in store for us, but for our descendants. But it is possible, through Christ, to break the chain and see the tide turn.

17. Read Ruth 1:1–5. How did Ruth, a Moabitess, come to be part of an Israelite family?

We know, from the rest of the story, that Ruth leaves the gods of Moab and puts her faith in the one true God. We also know, from Ephesians 1:4, that God chose those who would come to believe before the foundation of the world. If you are a believer who comes from a line of unbelievers, then you know God chose you—and like Ruth—part of His purpose for you may be in breaking the chain of sin of your ancestors. Ruth not only entered into the family of believers, she is one of the few women mentioned in the line of the Messiah (Matthew 1:5). Remember how God said no Moabite would enter in to the assembly of the Lord (Deuteronomy 23:3)? Ruth not only enters in, she becomes part of the holy line to the Messiah. Why? Because in God's eyes, she is no longer a Moabite—she is a new creation. She is a prefigures the new covenant that is open to all who believe, whether Jew or Gentile—no matter their past, no matter their sin—in Christ we can become new creations and be grafted into a vine that will bear beautiful fruit.

DAY 5

Risk Being a Ruth

No doubt about it—she was a risk taker. It takes faith that God exists and rewards those who diligently seek Him to take the kind of risks Ruth took. But oh! How He rewarded her. Not only was her own life transformed, but also her actions rippled out to generations to come.

If you grew up in an unbelieving family, you have much to learn from Ruth. But even if you were blessed to grow up in a believing family, every family has chinks in its coat of arms. Before we look at Ruth, we're going to ask you to consider those chinks.

Memory Work

Review your Memory Work.

Scripture Study

18. From what you know of your parents, grandparents, and great-grandparents, do

you see any unhealthy patterns that have come down through the family tree? Consider such things as addictions, abuse, sexual immorality, abandonment, legalism, materialism, divorce, abortion, and poor parenting.

We don't know anything about Ruth's personal history, only her corporate history as a Moabite. What we do see is that when given a choice to stay with the Moabites or go with Naomi to Bethlehem, she was amazingly courageous.

19. Read Ruth 1:6–18.

   A. Count how many times Naomi tries to send Ruth back to Moab in verses 8 through 15.

   B. Who goes back? Check your concordance to see if Orpah is ever mentioned again in the Bible. What significance do you see in this?

   C. Who takes the risk to go to Bethlehem? Find evidence in this passage for her faith in Naomi's God.

Naomi may have been the only believing woman who ever came across Ruth's path. Even though at this point she is bitter and hurting, Ruth is not going to leave her. Naomi was Ruth's hope for a better future for herself and her descendants.

20. Now, consider the weaknesses in your family chain. What woman do you know who exemplifies health and strength in these areas? How might you reach out to her?

21. If the sins of your forefathers have left you with emotional scars, what might you do

to seek Christian counseling?

22. Consider also your responsibility to be available to hurting women in your path, to help them break the chain. Note how Boaz was used of God to bring healing to Ruth. Find one or two principles in each passage that you might practice to also be a healer of broken hearts.

    A. Ruth 2:8–9

    B. Ruth 2:11

    C. Ruth 2:12

    D. Ruth 2:15–16

Of course, hidden in the figure of Boaz is Jesus, who is our kinsman-redeemer, and the best healer of our broken hearts.

23. Note also the part other believers played in Ruth's healing. What principles can you glean that you might practice to bring healing to someone like Ruth?

    A. Ruth 2:6

B. Ruth 3:1–4

C. Ruth 4:11–12

D. Ruth 4:14–15

24. As you are still before God, how would you apply today's lesson?

25. What do you think you will remember from this week's lesson? Why?

Prayer Time

All of the prayers in the book of Ruth are answered. Many were dramatic prayers of faith, such as praying that a barren woman would have a child who would become famous in Bethlehem! There is power in agreeing in prayer. When we are clean before the Lord and praying within His will, miracles can happen. If your group knows each other well, spend some time confessing your sins to one another, sharing the desires of your hearts, and praying for one another.

If your group is new and still building trust, go around and have each woman share one area where she would like to see growth in her life. Make note of what the woman on the right says and pray for her whenever she comes to mind.

Four

Mentoring Children

When my children were young I had so many natural opportunities to make a difference in the lives of their friends. That was especially true of the girls, whose friends seemed to soak up attention from an adult. Young hearts are tender, open, and malleable. I remember Tricia, the little girl who looked like Pippi Longstocking, with red braids, freckles, and an infectious grin. She lived next door and was a constant playmate of my daughter Sally. Tricia and Sally had their share of friendship troubles, as girls do, and we were constantly seeking biblical solutions together.

Tricia often joined us at our supper table, where we would act out Bible stories and proverbs. I remember the day Tricia put her faith in Christ. The girls were in the backseat of the car and I was doing errands. We were talking about spiritual things when all of a sudden I realized that Tricia had taken off her seatbelt and was kneeling in the backseat, praying to receive Christ. I said, "Wait, wait! Let me pull over!" I wanted to make sure she understood what she was doing. (She did!) Today Tricia is a woman who loves the Lord deeply and is serving Him as a nurse. Our large hospital just named her "Nurse of the Year" because of her Christlike compassion for her patients.

Now that my children are grown, I have opportunities with my grandchildren, neighborhood children, and children at church. There are a sea of children around you, longing for the love of an adult, whose hearts are open. How delighted they would be to have an adult take the initiative in a friendship. Shoot some hoops, bring the sidewalk chalk out, or set up a board game. That's all it takes! God has called us to bind up the broken-hearted, to reach out to the lost and lonely, and to mentor those who are in the household of faith. We also are practicing preventive medicine when we seize opportunities to train the next generation in healthy scriptural patterns of behavior. It is so much easier to train children how to walk on straight paths than to try to bring healing to their crippled state later in life.

Memory Work

Share with God's people who are in need. Practice hospitality.

Bless those who persecute you; bless and do not curse.

Romans 12:13–14

WARMUP

When you were a child, do you remember being with any adult Christians other than your parents (if your parents were Christians)? Who do you particularly remember and why? (Be brief.)

DAY I
. . . .

We Will Tell the Next Generation

The people that God delivered out of slavery in Egypt forgot His mighty miracles and were unfaithful to God. They rebelled against the laws and failed to pass on this mighty heritage to the next generation.

Yet there were those who stood in the gap—those who did reach out to children and told them of the wonders of God. For God has always needed faithful men and women to tell the next generation, has always needed them to stand in the gap so that He will have a remnant.

Memory Work

Review Romans 12:9–12.

Scripture Study

1. Read Psalm 78:1–8. Why are we to tell the next generation the praiseworthy deeds of the Lord?

2. Read Psalm 78:9–20 and describe the sin of the people. Find everything you can.

3. What are some praiseworthy deeds of the Lord that you could tell the next generation? Name two that have impacted your life from the Bible and two that stand out from your own life.

4. Who are some children that God has put in your path?

Personal Prayer Exercise

Write down the names of these children and pray for them, and pray that you will seize opportunities with them.

DAY 2
....
Teaching the Next Generation Effectively

Encouraging the next generation to turn to God with their problems is one of the most valuable lessons we can teach them. My friend Andrea tells the following story:

> When I was twelve, a good friend was being moody, and I told my mother: "Ashley is being a pill, so I'm going to be a pill to her so she can see what it feels like."
>
> Mother was quiet and finally said, "I know God has a different solution for you. He'll show you what it is, if you are alert."
>
> I said, "How will He show me?"
>
> Mother said, "I don't know. Maybe it will be through your devotional time. Maybe it will be when you are quiet in prayer. Maybe it will be another way. But if you ask Him, He will show you how He wants you to treat Ashley."
>
> The next day in Sunday school the lesson was on "A friend loves at all times." That was it! I was so excited to tell Mother that God had spoken to me!

Usually, God speaks through His Word. We must train our children to look to Scripture for solutions to problems. Two ways this can be accomplished are

1. Helping them become familiar with Scripture through memorization and study.

2. Going to Scripture for solutions when a problem comes up.

The proverbs are filled with practical advice for relationships. With my children, and now, with my grandchildren, we often come up with skits to illustrate the truths of proverbs. When doing a skit, keep it as simple as possible.

Memory Work

Begin memorizing Romans 12:13.

Scripture Study

*5. What do you think it means to "practice hospitality?"

6. How might you "practice hospitality" to children?

7. Come up with a simple skit for Romans 12:21. Put it in the scenario of children—where one child is unkind to another. How might the recipient of the unkindness "overcome evil with good?"

Child Evangelism holds to this practical truth: Children forget what they hear, they remember what they see, and they understand what they do. This is why acting out Bible stories and Bible truths is so helpful to children.

It is also important that, when telling Bible stories to children, they understand the meaning of the story and how it applies to them. The great preacher Charles Spurgeon commented that when we pass down the stories without the meaning, it is like passing down husks without the corn. Many children could tell you the story of David and Goliath or Noah's Ark—but they haven't a clue as to the meaning God intended for them to grasp or how to apply it to their lives.

8. Look at the following familiar Bible stories that children love to act out. It isn't enough for them to know what happened. After each story, state the meaning that you believe God intends. Then come up with an application that could be relevant to a child's life.

A. Matthew 7:24–27
   Central meaning

   Application for a child

B. Matthew 8:23–27
   Central meaning

   Application for a child

C. Matthew 18:21–35
   Central meaning

   Application for a child

DAY 3
Helping Girls Mature in Friendship

God calls the older women to mentor the younger women. That certainly includes children. As women we have experienced firsthand what it means to be a girl, and we can empathize with their needs and their hurts. Girls find their sense of identity in relationships, whereas boys are more likely to find their sense of identity in accomplishments.

I remember watching our then ten-year-old daughter, Annie, bond with a new friend. I watched with delight as the chemistry sparked between them. Within hours they were whispering together, conspiring, sharing secrets. They choreographed an elaborate dance to one of Amy Grant's songs, in which they held hands, swirled around each other, and swayed rhythmically together.

In the warmth of this new friendship, the smiles and glances at each other were abundant. The way that little girls play together is indicative of their gift for intimacy. Whereas the games of little boys tend to be competitive, putting feelings of self-worth ahead of relationships, the games of little girls tend to be relational. Little girls hold hands—they write love notes. They desire an intensity in their friendships that little boys prefer living without.

Yet the strength in the friendships of little girls also has a dark side, as they have a tendency toward dependency. They can do cruel things to protect their circle of two. They are also very vulnerable to peer pressure, to caving in to doing a wrong thing rather than losing fellowship with a group. They can join in gossip or press in too hard to a friend, smothering her.

Helping little girls to experience the reality of a vertical relationship with God is key to the health of their horizontal relationships. Though they are young, they can still learn about the reality not only of God, but also of the reality of their own deeply engraved sin nature, and their inability to conquer that sin without depending on the Holy Spirit.

When a girl experiences the painful consequences of sin, whether her own or another's cruelty, you will find her heart may be open to hearing scriptural truths. We have a responsibility to teach and to train so that the next generation may, indeed, mature in Christ.

Memory Work

Continue memorizing Romans 12:13–14.

Scripture Study

9. Read Jeremiah 17:5–9.

A. Why is it better, according to this passage, to find our security in God rather than in other people?

B. What is the difference between cherishing our friendships and depending on them for our emotional well-being?

C. How might a mother guide her daughter into having more than one close friend?

10. Read each of the following Proverbs passages and articulate its central truth. How might each apply to friendship?

A. Proverbs 3:27–28
Meaning

Friendship Application

B. Proverbs 4:23–27
Meaning

Friendship Application

C. Proverbs 11:13–14
   Meaning

Friendship Application

D. Proverbs 12:16–19
   Meaning

Friendship Application

E. Proverbs 13:20
   Meaning

Friendship Application

11. When you were a young girl, did you ever suffer because you expected a friend to always be there for you—and she wasn't?

Scripture tells us that David and Jonathan were soulmates. A soulmate is "a second self," someone who is very much like you. You can have more than one soulmate. "Best friend," however, connotes exclusivity. As girls mature in Christ, and learn to find their security in Him, they will become less grasping of their friends and more willing to give them breathing room. They will become more accepting of the idea of a few close friends rather than just one.

12. What practical things might a mother or other caring adult do to help the young girls in her life have more than one close friend?

DAY 4
Training and Role Playing

When I was a girl, my father would sometimes become angry with my childish and selfish choices. He would erupt, "Dee Dee—can't you just use your head?" I would be crushed. I also didn't know how to "just use my head." But one day, instead of responding to me with that angry question, he told me exactly what I had done wrong and how I could do it right. He said, "When your mother asks you to set the table, instead of getting up slowly with a sullen look on your face, I want you to say, 'Yes, Mother, I'd be glad to.' Then I want you to get up right away, cheerfully, and do it well."

That absolutely turned the light on for me—and I responded to it. Though the right behavior may be obvious to an adult, it isn't always to a child.

It may also be helpful to role play with a child. There are so many relational skills that can be improved through role play. Learning how to play the "hostess" in conversation, learning how to encourage without flattering, and learning how to stand up to a bully are just a few life situations we all need to be equipped to face. Role play with your child, niece, or young friend and you will be equipping them for life.

Memory Work

Continue your Memory Work.

Scripture Study

Read the following passages and reflect on the word "trained" or "training."

A student is not above his teacher, but everyone who is fully trained will be like his teacher. (Luke 6:40)

Everyone who competes in the games goes into strict training. They do it to get a crown that will not last; but we do it to get a crown that will last forever. (1 Corinthians 9:25)

Fathers, do not exasperate your children; instead, bring them up in the training and instruction of the Lord. (Ephesians 6:4)

13. How is an animal, an athlete, or a toddler well trained? In what ways might training be more extensive than teaching? (Use a dictionary if you are stumped!)

Teaching often involves telling, but training involves showing. It also involves repetition, correction, and practice!

14. Training often involves admonishing the negative and encouraging the positive. How do you see this in Ephesians 4:28–29?

15. Imagine that you have just heard your ten-year-old daughter yell unkindly at her younger sister for coming into her room without knocking. How might you seize this moment to train both girls? Write out your plan.

Role play is one effective way to train. For an effective apology, on the positive side, you

    A. go in person immediately if possible

    B. humbly own what you did wrong and how you realize it caused her pain

    C. make amends and/or assure her it won't happen again

    D. follow through

On the negative side, you do not

    A. let time pass

B. insinuate it is partly her fault (I'm sorry if I offended you)

C. make excuses for your behavior (Often there are extenuating circumstances, but still, what the hurt person wants to hear is your admission of sin—for though circumstances may make us more vulnerable to hurting others, there is still sin at the root.)

D. ignore the pain you've caused

E. fail to follow through with amends

16. Imagine that you simply forgot a lunch date with a friend and left her waiting for you. You arrive an hour late and she's gone. What would you do and say?

If you're role playing with a child, have your trainee make an apology for the same situation. Commend the good elements and point out the bad. Have her practice until it is exactly right. Next, see if she can apply these same principles to a different scenario: She borrowed a friend's sweater and washed it without looking at the label and it shrunk.

Action Assignment: Role play the above with a child and report what happened.

DAY 5
Walk in Dependence on the Lord

Each of us has a tendency toward idolatry. Just as it is dangerous to worship friends, so is it dangerous to worship ourselves. We are to cherish our friends, and even to cherish ourselves. We are fearfully and wonderfully made; God made us just a little lower than the angels. Yet the only One we can completely depend on is God.

It is vital that we realize that sin is deeply ingrained in us, so that we will constantly turn to the Lord. This is a lifelong lesson, but those who begin to see it when they are young are miles ahead.

How do we depend on God in our daily life? The holy habits of Bible reading, prayer, and worship are vehicles of His grace, but the discipline that has helped me the most is learning to walk in daily repentance. Though I am fearfully and wonderfully made, I am also fallen—and sin is deep within me. I easily move out of the light on a daily basis. When I do this, I walk away from fellowship with God because He will not go with me into the darkness. I still have a relationship with Him, and He will never leave me nor forsake me, but I don't have His peace, His joy, or His power.

If I could train the next generation in only one thing, it would be to walk in continual repentance. Learning to recognize the prompting of the Holy Spirit and responding to Him is key in living a life of dependence on God.

Review Romans 12:9–14.

17. Read 1 John 1:5–9.

 A. What truth do you learn about God in 1 John 1:5?

 B. In order to have fellowship with God, what must we not do? (1 John 1:6)

When we walk into darkness, we do not lose our relationship with God, but we do lose fellowship, for He will not follow us into sin.

 C. How does walking in the light affect our relationships with one another? (1 John 1:7)

 D. What must we realize is ingrained within us? (1 John 1:8)

 E. Describe the promise and condition of 1 John 1:9. Is this the practice of your daily life?

 F. Confess your sins to God now. How will you do a U-turn? Be specific.

G. Would the next generation be aware of your walking in repentance? If so, how?

18. What do you think you will remember from this week's lesson? Why? How will you apply it to your life?

Prayer Time

Break into groups of three or four. Each woman should take a turn sharing her answer to the last question and then the others can support her. Then go around again, giving women the opportunity to share another request and receive support.

Five

Honoring Family Bonds

When my sisters and I were young, and squabbling, my dad would sit us down and talk to us tenderly. He would say, "You are sisters. Please, let's not have fighting between you."

One mother told her quarreling adult children: "Daddy's gone. One day I'll be too. You are the only ones who have each other from the cradle to the grave." How true.

A woman named Jan e-mailed me, saying,

> When Mother died, it was a great comfort to be with my older brother and sister, to be with the people grieving the same loss I was. I had a real sense of going through that family crisis together. And a week later, when Christmas came, I realized that even with my mother gone (the woman who "made" Christmas for us all) I still had family to come home to. And I know we'll continue to get together even after my father dies. At times like this, I'm glad I'm not an only child.

Families are a gift from God. Of course, as believers, we have another family, the family of God. But Scripture is clear that we are to value our biological family as well.

Memory Work

Rejoice with those who rejoice; mourn with those who mourn. Live in harmony with one another. Do not be proud, but be willing to associate with people of low position. Do not be conceited.

Romans 12:15–16

WARMUP

Have each woman share how she hopes she will be treated by her family if she becomes an old woman. What would be particularly important to her?

DAY I
. . . .

How Good and How Pleasant It Is

Family bonds are important. The familiar (not scriptural) proverb "blood is thicker than water" refers to the strength of family bonds, indicating that they surpass the bonds of friendship. The blood of the covenant can actually be stronger than the blood of genetics. Yet, still, biological bonds *are* strong and Scripture clearly values the biological family. The Lord urges harmony and responsibility within the biological family as well as the covenant family.

Memory Work

Begin your Memory Work of Romans 12:15.

Scripture Study

1. Read Genesis 13:8–9. What was happening and what argument did Abram make to Lot for ending the problem?

2. Read Psalm 133.

   A. With what statement does this psalm open?

   B. Two word pictures are then given to illustrate the beauty of family harmony. What is the first, in verse 2?

* C. What do you associate with the above picture? Think about fragrance, diffusive-ness, and the purpose of the oil—how might this help you understand how God views family harmony?

D. What is the second word picture to illustrate the beauty of family harmony given in verse 3?

* E. What do you associate with dew coming down from a mountain? What is its effect, and what is the point of the descent from higher elevations?

3. Write down some of the reasons you are thankful for your parents and siblings. If they are completely dysfunctional and only brought you pain, then write down some of the reasons you are thankful for spiritual parents and siblings.

4. If there is someone in your family with whom you are not at peace, how might you apply Romans 12:18?

DAY 2
....
Honor Your Father and Your Mother

When I was a little girl, my grandmother told me not to call my mother "Mom" but "Mother" as a sign of honor. I almost always did. For me, it was relatively easy to honor my father and my mother, for each was an individual worthy of great respect. They each had strong qualities of integrity, compassion, and honesty. I realize not all children are so blessed—and yet that does not invalidate God's command. As with government leaders, whether or not we respect them as people, we are to show respect for the position they hold and the fact that God, in His sovereignty, allowed them that position.

Memory Work

Continue memorizing Romans 12:15.

Scripture Study

5. Write out the commandment and promise of Exodus 20:5.

6. What do Proverbs 30:11 and 30:17 say?

This is an account, Matthew Henry explains, of some wicked generations "that are justly abominable to all that are virtuous and good. [They] are abusive to their parents, give them bad language and wish them ill, call them bad names and actually injure them...." This generation actually mocks their parents, and Matthew Henry notes that God sees the mocking or leering eye. The doom of those "eyes" is likened to the doom of the eyes of criminals who are hung and whose eyes are then vulnerable to birds of prey (*Matthew Henry's Commentary*, #3, Hendrickson, 1991, pp. 796-797).

7. Read Genesis 9:20–27.

   A. What happened in verse 21?

   B. Describe how Ham treated his father.

C. Describe how Shem and Japheth treated him.

D. What prophecy is Noah given?

* E. What meaning for us do you see recorded in this story?

Some might say that because Noah allowed himself to get drunk, he was not worthy of honor. But God's command does not change. Even when our parents behave poorly, we are to treat them with respect and honor. This doesn't mean we are to support destructive habits, or that we cannot protect ourselves or our children from abuse, but that we are always to show our parents respect. God has placed them over us. The root word for "honor" is derived from the word "heavy." Someone to be honored is someone of weight in God's eyes. When something weighty is treated as if it were light, as the above story of Ham illustrates, this is an abomination to God.

8. What does honoring your parents look like? What does dishonoring them look like?

DAY 3
. . . .
Obedience versus Honor

When we are in the season of childhood, Scripture is clear. We are not only to honor, but also to obey our parents. To obey is to do what someone asks. What about honor? To honor is to treat someone with the weighty respect they deserve—but that may or may not include obedience.

So the next question is, at what point do we move from obedience to honor? At what point does childhood end?

Some would say it is when children leave the home, yet in biblical times adult children may have lived with their parents and helped in an agrarian culture. Today, marriage doesn't seem to necessarily be a logical dividing point, for those children who do not marry still become adults. Many children leave home but are still financially dependent. Perhaps the clearest dividing line would be when the child is carrying his full weight financially.

On the subject of marrying, J. Douma, professor of ethics from the Reformed Theological Seminary of the Netherlands, comments on choosing a marriage partner, in which some children would say a parent should not participate. He says that older commentaries on the fifth commandment discuss the task of a parent concerning his child's courtship and marriage, and that 1 Corinthians 7:25–40 specifically discusses a father giving or not giving his daughter in marriage. Douma writes,

> Children are not honoring their parents by treating courtship and marriage as strictly private matters beyond parental control. Serious dating means the child is preparing to "leave his father and mother" (Gen. 2:24), and parents should be able to talk with their children about this departure…. Nowadays parents do not choose marriage partners for their children. But they still have a right to be involved in the choice. That right becomes all the stronger if they see their son or daughter taking a wrong spiritual turn in dating. (*The Ten Commandments*, R&R Publishing, 1996, p. 174)

When parents stand in opposition to God's Word, then a child is free to disobey, just as Peter disobeyed the political leaders who told him to preach about Christ. Some parents will ask a child to renounce Christ or not to marry someone because they are a strong Christian. In these cases we are to obey God rather than man. Sometimes we are called, as were Abraham and Ruth, to leave our father's house, so that we can become part of a godly seed.

Memory Work

Review Romans 12:15 and begin learning Romans 12:16.

Scripture Study

9. What does Ephesians 6:1–3 say?

10. How would you differentiate between obedience and honor? When do you think a person passes from childhood to adulthood?

11. What thoughts do you have on Professor J. Douma's comments on parental involvement in the choice of a marriage partner? Why?

12. King Lemuel's mother instructed him on the taking of a wife. What kind of women, according to Proverbs 31:1–3, did she advise him to avoid?

13. What kind of wife did she tell him to seek? (Proverbs 31:10–11; 31:30)

DAY 4
Honoring Elderly Parents

Leviticus 19:32 says, "Rise in the presence of the aged, show respect for the elderly and revere your God. I am the Lord." In many cultures, honoring the elderly is beautifully observed. Their years of experience and wisdom are valued. But in many western civilizations, the elderly are not honored. Our culture values youth and beauty, not wisdom. May we give the elderly the weight God gives them and honor them, remembering that we, if God grants us life, will be elderly too.

Memory Work

Complete memorizing Romans 12:15–16.

Scripture Study

14. Read 1 Timothy 5:1–8.

   A. What analogies are made between family bonds and the family of God in verses 1–2?

B. What instruction is given to children and grandchildren of widows in verse 4?

C. What strong statement is made in verse 8?

"Anyone" is not gender specific in the Greek, so it refers to both males and females. "Providing" definitely enters the financial realm but extends to emotional support as well.

D. If you have a widowed parent or grandparent, how are you showing them support?

15. What additional reason is given to support widows in 1 Timothy 5:16?

Widows in biblical times had dire needs because they could not own property. Yet though their position may be better today, the principle of caring for widows in your family still stands.

16. How does James 1:27 define "true religion"?

17. How did Jesus rebuke the Pharisees in Matthew 15:3–9?

18. If the Lord grants you life and you experience old age and the deterioration of your

body, how do you hope your children and family will respond to you? Be specific.

19. How would you apply today's lesson to your life?

DAY 5
Honoring Our Brother

After Cain, out of jealousy, had carried out the planned murder of his brother, God came to Cain and asked,

> *Where is your brother Abel?*
>
> Genesis 4:9a

Disrespectfully and infamously, Cain replied,

> *I don't know. Am I my brother's keeper?*
>
> Genesis 4:9b

Charles Spurgeon said,

> To what a shameful pitch of presumptuous impudence had Cain arrived when he could thus insult the Lord God.... Men blaspheme frightfully, but it is usually because they forget God, and ignore his presence; but Cain was conscious that God was speaking to him.... The cool impudence of Cain is an indication of the state of heart which led up to his murdering his brother. (The C.H. Spurgeon Collection, Ages Software, 1998, Sermon #1399)

God calls us to love one another, to honor one another—and the New Testament warns us, "Do not be like Cain ..." (1 John 3:12). Today's closing Scriptures show us how important it is to God that we love and honor our brothers, and how wise we are if we respond to the first prompting of the Spirit that lets us know we have wandered into the dark.

Memory Work

Review Romans 12:15–16.

Scripture Study

20. Read Genesis 4:1–12.

A. Describe the offerings of Cain and Abel.

B. What was God's response to each?

Cain's choosing an easier offering was indicative of his evil heart, and God could see that. He also foreshadowed the type of person who wants to do things his own way instead of God's way. God says that "without the shedding of blood there is no forgiveness" (Hebrews 9:22).

C. How did Cain respond to God's displeasure?

It is always easier to repent sooner than later, for each time we refuse to respond to the Spirit, we grow harder. It becomes harder to hear, harder to yield. It is though a callous grows on our heart.

D. How does God entreat Cain? What is the promise and what is the warning of Genesis 4:6–7?

E. What similar warning are we given in Ephesians 4:27? What do you think this means?

F. How did Cain respond to God's entreaty? (Genesis 4:8)

G. Count how many times the word "brother" occurs in Genesis 4:8–11. Do you see any significance in this? If so, what?

21. Is the Spirit prompting you concerning a relationship in your life? Be still. Write down anything He brings to mind.

22. What do you think you will remember from this week's lesson? Why?

Prayer Time

Break into groups of three or four. Begin with thanksgiving for family bonds. Then each woman should lift up the need of her heart and allow her sisters to support her with sentence prayers.

Six

Overcoming Adult Sibling Rivalry

Michael Kahn and Dr. Stephen Bank, authors of *The Sibling Bond* (Basic Books, 1982), write, "There is growing evidence that siblings provide a highly supportive social network in old age when spouses die, and children have gone their separate ways." Even those who have siblings, however, may be lonely if they cannot outgrow rivalry.

Whether your siblings are in your family or in the body of Christ, overcoming rivalry is key to relating to them in a joyful way. *Rivalry* in Latin means "having rights to the same stream." For siblings, that stream is the parents' love and approval. Nearly all siblings have it. For some, rivalry is exacerbated through parental favoritism. Kahn says parents who played favorites "can reach back from the grave, leaving a bitter legacy" to children who cannot reconcile. Yet, in Christ, it is possible for even these children to overcome their rivalry.

Memory Work

> *Do not repay anyone evil for evil. Be careful to do what is right in the eyes of everyone. If it is possible, as far as it depends on you, live at peace with everyone.*
> Romans 12:17–18

WARMUP

Have each woman share briefly the value of brothers and sisters—in the family and the family of God. For what is she particularly thankful?

DAY 1
Parental Favoritism

In an earlier lesson we looked at how the sins of the fathers are passed down from one generation to the next. Isaac (who had been his parent's favorite) showed favoritism to his son Esau. Rebekah, his wife, favored Jacob. One day Jacob favored his son Joseph—which led to one of the ugliest episodes of sibling rivalry in Scripture.

Memory Work

Review Romans 12:9–16.

Scripture Study

1. Read Genesis 25:21–28.

   A. How did God answer Isaac's prayer? (v. 21)

   B. What question did Rebekah have of the Lord, and what was His answer? (vv. 22–23)

   C. Describe each parent's favorite twin and the reason for each one's favorite. (vv. 27–28)

Authors Kahn and Bank explain in *The Sibling Bond* that parental favoritism is a key factor in fueling lifelong sibling rivalry. They explain,

> Favoritism occurs in all families, but in well-functioning families, children are favored for different characteristics or at different periods in their life ... so that on the whole no child clearly prevails.

2. Read Genesis 27.

A. What was Isaac's plan and how did his wife, Rebekah, respond? What evidence do you see for a lack of fear of God in her? (vv. 1–13)

B. Describe what happened. (vv. 14–33)

C. Describe Esau's response in verse 34.

D. Have you ever felt as Esau did—longing for the blessing of a parent? If so, share something about it.

E. What was Esau's response to Jacob? (v. 41)

F. What did Rebekah do? (vv. 42–45)

Rebekah never sees Jacob again in her earthly life.

3. How would you advise someone who felt he or she was deprived of his or her parents' blessing to get past the pain and on to healthy relationships, not only with siblings, but with everyone?

4. If you are a mother, grandmother, or aunt—what are some things you do (or avoid doing) to balance the love and acceptance you give your children?

DAY 2

Forgiving Our Brothers

Forgiveness isn't natural. When someone hurts you, when someone seems unrepentant, the natural response is to want to hurt back, or at the very least, withdraw. It isn't natural to forgive. It's supernatural.

"A lack of forgiveness," it has been said, "is a poison we drink hoping others will die."

How sad to see families divided—parent, child; brother, sister. If family harmony is sweet to God, how these grudges and graceless lives must grieve His heart.

Memory Work

Begin memorizing Romans 12:17.

Scripture Study

5. Read Matthew 18:21–35.

    A. What question did Peter have for Jesus?

    B. What happened in the story Jesus told?

    C. Who does the king represent? Who does the first servant represent? And the second?

D. What is the point of the story?

6. What does Ephesians 4:32 say?

7. If our brother is not repentant, must we still forgive him? Why? (Consider this week's memory passage.)

Sometimes Christians feel that a brother must be repentant before we can forgive, but truly, that is God's right to demand, not ours.

Sometimes Christians confuse forgiveness and drawing boundaries. You can forgive your brother from your heart and still, if he is unrepentant, put some protective space between the two of you. David, for example, forgave King Saul from his heart for his repeated murder attempts, but he still put space between himself and the king.

DAY 3
· ·
How to Respond to Pain in Relationships

Henry Brandt, who has spent much of his life working with lepers, often speaks of the gift of pain. If lepers felt pain, they would know to withdraw their fingers from being burned, their toes from hitting sharp rocks. Instead, they lose their fingers, toes ...

How we respond to pain indicates much about our spiritual sensitivity. If we deny our pain or blame others, never allowing God's light to search our own heart, we may lose a friend, a brother, and certainly the joy and peace of fellowship with God.

Pain is a gift from God. We shouldn't deny it, but respond to it. Our Father who loves us has allowed it for our good.

Memory Work

Complete your Memory Work of Romans 12:17.

Scripture Study

8. Read Hebrews 12:5–13.

   A. What shouldn't we do and why when the Lord disciplines us? (vv. 5–6)

   B. Why does God discipline us? (vv. 7–10)

   C. When we are experiencing the discipline of God, or even our own discipline in desiring to form holy habits, what must we keep in mind, according to verse 11?

9. What was the first consequence of sin that Jacob experienced? (Genesis 27:43–44)

10. What was the advice of Jesus to those who become aware that their brother has something against them? (Matthew 5:23–24)

11. Can you share a time when you humbled yourself and went to your brother and confessed your sin? What happened?

DAY 4
· ·

The Goodness of God

Jacob is running, running, running. Finally, exhausted, he lies down to sleep with a stone for a pillow. There he has an encounter with the living God.

Memory Work

Begin memorizing Romans 12:18.

Scripture Study

12. Read Genesis 28:10–22.

    A. Describe the dream Jacob had. What promises did God give him?

    B. How do you see the goodness of God in the above?

    C. According to Romans 2:4, how should the goodness of God impact us?

    * D. How do you see Jacob "bargaining" with God in Genesis 28:16–22? What does he want God to do for him? What does he say he will do in return?

    E. What wrong heart attitude do you see in Jacob?

13. Have you ever tried to bargain with God? What is flawed in this kind of thinking?

DAY 5
Over the Potter's Wheel

God's purpose for us is to be holy. We are His children, and He will discipline us. When He allows pain in our lives, and often that pain comes through relationships, He may be trying to get our attention. If we ignore Him or resist Him, He won't give up. Instead, the fire increases. It certainly did for Jacob. How skillfully God designed the discipline, just as a Master Potter would. He knew exactly where Jacob's rough spots were and the Lord turned him over the fire, to melt the clay so that His hands could smooth His very chipped pot.

Memory Work

Complete your memorization of Romans 12:17–18.

Scripture Study

14. Read Genesis 29:1–25.

A. How did Jacob respond upon meeting Rachel? Why, do you think?

B. What did Laban say that must have warmed Jacob's heart? (Genesis 29:13–14)

C. What bargain did Laban and Jacob strike? (Genesis 29:15–20)

D. What did Jacob say to Laban in Genesis 29:21? What do you think of his words?

E. Describe how Laban tricked Jacob. How did he get away with it?

F. Put yourself in Jacob's place. Why might this have been not only disappointing, but humiliating?

G. What similarities can you find between the way Jacob tricked Esau and the way Laban tricked Jacob?

H. In reflecting over your life, can you think of times when you hurt others through deceitfulness, betrayal, or immorality of some kind? You don't need to share this in the group, and you may want to write your answer on a separate sheet of paper. Confess these things to God, and then burn or shred or tear up the paper.

I. Now, can you think of ways that others have hurt you through the same kind of sins that you have inflicted on others? Did God teach you anything through this? If you haven't reflected on this—do so now. Recall some of the feelings you had as a result of this person's sin. Ask yourself two things:
   1. What has this shown you about your sin?

2. Has this increased the grace you give to others when they sin?

Spend some time in personal prayer for your character, that His Spirit might remind you before you hurt others with sin or a lack of grace.

Prayer Time

Break into groups of three or four. Each woman should lift up the need of her heart and allow her sisters to support her with sentence prayers.

Seven

Hope for Fractured Families

The longitudinal studies of the effects of divorce on children are sobering. A child of divorce is severely traumatized and the effects last throughout his life. Judith Wallerstein, widely considered a foremost authority on children of divorce, was one of the key researchers for the book *The Unexpected Legacy of Divorce: A 25 Year Landmark Study*. Many have the attitude that because divorce is so common, it is no big deal. Yet Wallerstein says, "People who believe that numbers mute the individual child's suffering have simply not talked to the children. Each child in a classroom half full of children of divorce cries out, 'Why me?'" ... Moreover, contrary to what we have long thought, the major impact of divorce does not occur during childhood or adolescence. Rather, it arises in adulthood as serious romantic relationships move center stage. When it comes time to choose a life mate and build a new family, the effects of divorce crescendo (Hyperion, 2000, XXVIII, XXIX).

We will begin this week with the story of Rachel and Leah, two sisters who suffered the traumatic effects of polygamy. Our contemporary parallel is divorce—instead of several wives at a time, it is one wife after another. The effects on the children of having multiple parents can be similar. The traumatic childhoods of the children of Rachel and Leah (and Zilpah and Bilhah) are indicative of what happens, long-term, to children who have negative role models. In this family, the lack of healthy relationships not only continued but increased. When you consider Joseph and his brothers, you see increased favoritism, bickering, and violence.

Is there any hope? Yes—yes! There is great hope in Christ. Whether you are a victim of divorce or are one who could offer a bridge over troubled water, Scripture provides the wisdom we need.

I want to make it clear that this lesson is not about heaping blame on the divorced. First of all, as next week will show, there are times when healthy boundaries to an abusive or an addicted mate will lead to divorce. That's a necessary risk at times. There are also innocent victims of divorce: wives who did want their husbands to leave, the children, and the grandchildren. Even if a divorce was due to sin on the part of the reader, who of us can cast the first stone? This lesson is not about heaping blame on victims, but on discovering ways to be helped and to help others.

Memory Work

> *Do not take revenge, my friends, but leave room for God's wrath, for it is written: "It is mine to avenge; I will repay," says the Lord.*
> Romans 12:19

WARMUP

Go around the room and ask each woman to share what situations tend to be fertile soil for jealousy for them. They may pass if they choose.

DAY 1
. . . .
Leah

Though Jacob matured in the Lord, he was not able to break the chain of playing favorites. Rachel was his favorite wife—the woman he truly wanted to marry. It had to be demoralizing to be the less beautiful sister, the less loved wife, and the mother of the less loved children.

Leah has lessons to teach us. We have all experienced Leah-like moments, though perhaps not to her intensity. If we have been denied one of the greatest desires of our hearts (marriage, motherhood, or love from a parent or spouse) it can be spiritually challenging to rejoice along with those who have been blessed with those gifts. Yet trusting the Lord and knowing He loves us and has a plan for us, too, can help us overcome jealousy. Leah makes a beginning step toward being emotionally healthier after the birth of her fourth son.

Memory Work

Review Romans 12:9–18.

Scripture Study

1. Try to imagine how you might have felt if you had been Leah in each of the following circumstances.

    A. Genesis 29:16–17

    B. Genesis 29:25–30

    C. Genesis 29:31–35

2. According to the names of her first three sons, what seemed to be Leah's greatest desire?

3. Describe Jacob's love for Rachel using whatever you can find in the Scripture. Using your imagination, describe what might have been some difficult situations for Leah.

* 4. What change do you see in Leah in Genesis 29:35? How was this a beginning step toward health?

5. God is looking for those who love Him for who He is, not just for what He can give. This is a key principle for spiritual health. How do you see Habakkuk coming to this same point in Habakkuk 3:17–19?

DAY 2
• •
Rachel

She was the wife who was loved. Yet she too was miserable. The greatest desire of her heart was to have children. Her sister had little boys clinging to her skirts, but Rachel's womb was barren.

When Rachel had Jacob take a concubine so that she could have children through her, she said, "I have had a great struggle with my sister, and I have won" (Genesis 30:8). In reality no one won—for both sisters' lives were a trail of sorrow.

Rachel didn't do as well as Leah in overcoming her sorrow. As we look at her life, we get some clues as to why she failed to attain the kind of spiritual health that leads to peace and joy.

Memory Work

Begin memorizing Romans 12:19.

Scripture Study

6. Read Genesis 30:1–7.

   A. How does Jacob respond to Rachel's anger in Genesis 30:1–2?

   B. What does Rachel name her sons through Bilhah. What insight does this give you into her?

7. Read Genesis 30:14–20. (There was an "old wives' tale" that said that mandrakes made a woman fertile.)

   A. What accusation does Leah level toward Rachel?

87

B. How does Rachel then show Leah she has the upper hand?

C. Find evidence for God's compassion to each woman despite her twisted perspective and sinful attitude. Give Scripture references.

8. When Jacob is ready to flee his deceitful father-in-law with his wives and children, we are given a glimpse into the feelings that the sisters had for their father and why. What do you discover in Genesis 31:14–18?

9. How might this lack of parental love have shaped their individual characters? What might have helped these women? (Review lesson 3.)

10. What does Rachel do in Genesis 31:19? What does this tell you about her?

When Laban comes rushing after them in a rage, Rachel hides these gods under her skirts. Leslie Williams, in *Seduction of the Lesser Gods,* writes,

> Without knowing fully what we are doing, we hide the things we secretly love and admire under our skirts, like Rachel, sitting primly and righteously on our camels, wondering why we are not whole, why we still suffer, why we are not reconciled to the God we profess. (Word, 1997, p. 12)

11. What "lesser gods" (things that you secretly love and admire) do you hide under your skirts? Would you be willing to forsake them so that you can be reconciled to the God you profess?

DAY 3

The Wife-in-Law

If your children have a step-mother, or if you are a step-mother to another woman's children, then you have what author Ann Cryster calls "a wife-in-law." She is the other woman who is involved intimately with your family. How you relate to her will affect not only your own health, but also the health of your children. One ex-wife tells of her feelings upon meeting the new wife:

> I was working around the house that afternoon. Hank, Trish, and the kids had been away for Labor Day, and they suddenly pulled into the driveway. After eight hours in the car, Trish hops out in perfectly pressed linen shorts with every hair on her head in place. I felt like Godzilla facing Venus. It was the first time I had seen them as a couple, a family. I thought I had a grip on it all, but when I went back into the house I cried for the entire night. I can't describe the loneliness, the unhappiness. I was convinced that no one would ever love me again. I felt used up, discarded and ridiculous. (*The Wife-in-law Trap*, Pocket Star Books, 1990, pp. 15–16)

The ex-wife has to deal with the pain of feeling discarded. The new wife has the challenge of dealing with the fact that her husband may miss his first wife and that there are ways she may not measure up. The children often become the pawns, carriers of information and emotion.

Learning to forgive, to find our love in the Lord, and to overcome evil with good are keys to this extremely painful situation.

Memory Work

Continue memorizing Romans 12:19.

Scripture Study

12. When Hagar literally was "discarded" in the desert, what gave her hope? (Review lesson 3.)

Though I know the pain of a divorcee is unique from the pain of a widow, there are similarities. When I start to think, *Who really loves me now that Steve is gone?* I remind myself that God does. When I think, *Oh, I wish Steve were here to share this sunset, this Christmas, this grand-baby's smile....* I remind myself that my heavenly Husband is sharing these moments with me, and as the Master Designer behind them all, delights in my delight. When I think, *If only I could talk to Steve,* I remind myself that God is just waiting to dialogue with me, and so I pour out my heart to Him and then quiet my soul so that I can listen.

13. Read Psalm 34 and write down some of the word pictures that minister to you. Why do you find them meaningful?

Ann Cryster says the two most common obstacles she found that kept a woman from overcoming a negative relationship with her wife-in-law were the inability to forgive and the inability to conquer the debilitating emotions of jealousy, resentment, and bitterness. One woman wrote,

> I had lost my mate, and to some extent my social position. I know my wife-in-law [husband's new wife] is much better off financially than I am. She's the one taking the fancy trips and redecorating her home while I'm pinching pennies. But one thing I wasn't prepared for was my five-year-old daughter coming to me one day and saying, "Oh, Mommy, Mara makes the best fried chicken, and we had so much fun planting a garden together. I can't wait to go back next Saturday." (*The Wife-in-law Trap*, Pocket Star Books, 1990, p. 20)

14. Review Romans 12:9–21. How might the above woman talk to her soul, using Scripture to help her to face a challenging situation in a healing way?

DAY 4
Damage Control for Children of Divorce

Two factors can have a dramatic impact in breaking the chain: genuine forgiveness and positive role models. Tomorrow we'll look at Joseph and how he was able to forgive his family and break the chain.

Today, consider the enormous impact of role models. Many children of divorce choose very unwisely when it comes to a spouse—sometimes choosing someone whom they think is inferior enough to them that they will never leave. Children of divorce are much more apt to divorce themselves at the first sign of trouble. But if they see a different kind of home, a committed marriage full of love and grace, it can absolutely be a beacon to them through troubled waters.

If you are a victim of divorce, I urge you to seek out godly role models. If you are not a victim of divorce, I urge you to practice hospitality toward those who are.

Memory Work

Complete your Memory Work of Romans 12:19.

Scripture Study

15. What is the key thought concerning hospitality that you find in Luke 14:12–14?

Our Lord is not meaning that we should not be hospitable to family and friends, but that our motive should be to help and not to be looking for something in return. If you have been blessed with a strong marriage, you can do a lot of good by having single-parent families over, by reaching out to fatherless children, and by having younger couples over.

16. Read Isaiah 58:6–7. How does the Lord define "true spirituality"? What application might there be toward children (of any age) of divorce?

If you are a single mom, you may need to take the initiative. You may need to go to some of the strong families in your church and tell them of your need. You could say something like, "I've been reading about the long-term impact of divorce on children. Because they haven't seen positive role models in marriage, they fear marriage, they make bad choices in mates, and they divorce easily. I so long for my children to see some positive role models. I want them to sit at a supper table, or play a board game, or go camping with a godly family. Could you pray about it and see if there's any way you might provide that for my children sometimes?"

17. If you are a single mom, consider the above and then write out your own paragraph—something that you might feel comfortable saying to a couple.

You can also pray for your children, for God hears the fervent prayers of a righteous man or woman. Do you remember Jochebed and Moses? She had to give her son to a pagan Egyptian family. (Some of you have to see your children go, every other week, or weekend, into your divorced spouse's home, which may be a godless home.) I believe Jochebed prayed for her son. Look at what happened—at what I believe was an answer to Jochebed's prayers.

18. Read Exodus 2:11–25.

A. Describe Moses' sin and the evidence that he knew he was doing wrong. (Exodus 2:11–14) Why, according to your Memory Work, was this wrong?

Pastor Tom Nelson commented that Moses, having grown up in the lap of luxury, seemed to have become proud. God was going to use the wilderness to humble him, but also a hospitable home—a Gentile home with a God-fearing man named Jethro. Time spent in the wilderness and in this home transformed Moses. (Series on Moses, Summer of 2006, Christ Community Church, Olathe, Kansas.)

B. How did Moses behave gallantly toward the daughters of Jethro? (Exodus 2:16–17)

C. When the daughters rushed home with the story, what question and command did Jethro have for his daughters? (vv. 18–20)

D. How did Jethro's invitation extend beyond a meal? (v. 21)

19. Read Exodus 18. Then, with scriptural support, write down what you learn about Jethro's character and wisdom.

20. What does the Lord say about Moses in Numbers 12:2–9? What transformation do you see in his character? What factors transformed him, do you think?

DAY 5
● ●
Breaking the Cycle of Ungrace

Jacob and Esau didn't reconcile until they were old men, and the evidence is that though they were reconciled, they were not close.

Rachel and Leah bickered until death parted them.

The sons of Leah and the sons of Rachel were at odds, resulting in one of the ugliest episodes of sibling rivalry in history. Leah's sons not only threw Rachel's son Joseph into a pit, they sold him into slavery, and lied to their father, saying he had been slain by a wild animal.

You may be very familiar with the famous story of Joseph forgiving his brothers, but what I'd like you to discover today is how forgiveness brought health to an extremely dysfunctional family.

Memory Work

Review Romans 12:9–19.

Scripture Study

We begin our story at the scene where Joseph's brothers have gone to Egypt for help in a time of famine. They do not know that their brother, whom they sold into slavery, is now the right-hand man to the Pharaoh.

21. Read Genesis 41:41–57.

   A. Describe Joseph's position. (Genesis 41:41–44)

   B. What did Joseph do, by faith, to provide for the coming famine? (vv. 46–49)

93

C. What did Joseph name his sons and why? (vv. 50–52) What do these names indicate about Joseph's steps toward recovery?

22. Read Genesis 42—46 as if it were a novel. There are twists and turns in Joseph's forgiving his brothers—it's an emotional roller coaster. Describe the events leading up to the reconciliation.

Now read Philip Yancey's illuminating comments on the passage you've just read:

> When I was a child listening to the story in Sunday school, I could not understand the loops and twists in the account of Joseph's reconciliation with his brothers. One moment Joseph acted harshly, throwing his brothers in jail; the next moment he seemed overcome with sorrow, leaving the room to blubber like a drunk. He played tricks on his brothers, hiding money in their grain sacks, seizing one as a hostage, accusing another of stealing his silver cup. For months, maybe years, these intrigues dragged on until finally Joseph could restrain himself no longer. He summoned his brothers and dramatically forgave them.
>
> I now see that story as a realistic depiction of the unnatural act of forgiveness. The brothers Joseph struggled to forgive were the very ones who had bullied him, had cooked up schemes to murder him, had sold him into slavery. Because of them he had spent the best years of his youth moldering in an Egyptian dungeon. Though he went on to triumph over adversity and though with all his heart he now wanted to forgive these brothers, he could not bring himself to that point, not yet. The wound still hurt too much....
>
> When grace finally broke through to Joseph, the sound of his grief and love echoed throughout the palace. What is that wail? Is the king's minister sick? No, Joseph's health was fine. It was the sound of a man forgiving.
>
> Behind every act of forgiveness lies a wound of betrayal, and the pain of being betrayed does not easily fade away. (*What's So Amazing About Grace?*, Zondervan, 1997, pp. 84-85)

23. Read Genesis 45:1–2. What happened? Comment on Yancey's interpretation.

24. Read Genesis 45:14–15 and describe the scene.

25. What key to Joseph's spiritual recovery do you find in Genesis 50:20?

26. Is there someone you need to forgive? Are you willing to make the sacrifice of letting him off the hook? Why must we, according to Matthew 18:34–35?

27. What do you think you will remember from this week's lesson? How might you apply it?

Prayer Time

Break into groups of three or four. Each woman should lift up the need of her heart and allow her sisters to support her with sentence prayers.

Eight

Boundaries for Health*

The caller was in tears. She'd been listening to the radio as Dr. John Townsend, coauthor of *Boundaries*, explained why we must not support the unhealthy choices of those we love, but must instead draw boundaries so that they can experience the natural consequences of poor choices. She said, "I've done everything wrong. I'm taking care of my daughter's baby while she is running around, sleeping wherever, and abusing me with language and hatred. But if I don't do the things she wants, she says I'll never see my granddaughter again" (Mid-Day Connection, Moody Radio, September, 2006).

Townsend asked the woman a few questions and discovered that if she didn't care for her granddaughter then the baby would go to live with her father, who would take good care of her. Then Townsend said, "You need to stop trying to hold onto your daughter. Let her go. Let her experience the consequences of her choices."

Townsend also told of parents of a grown son coming to him. They were providing everything for their son while he sat home watching television, drinking, and making a mess. They wanted the counselor to "fix" their son. They were astonished when he told them that their son didn't have a problem. "He doesn't have a problem because you have taken it from him.... Would you like me to help you help him have some problems?" (*Boundaries*, Zondervan, 1992, p. 28).

Boundaries are needed for healthy relationships—not just in parenting, but in marriage, in friendship, and in all human relationships.

Memory Work

On the contrary: "If your enemy is hungry, feed him; if he is thirsty, give him something to drink. In doing this, you will heap burning coals on his head." Do not be

96

overcome by evil, but overcome evil with good.

Romans 12:20–21

WARMUP

What are some reasons Christians might be uncomfortable with setting boundaries? Are you? Comment.

DAY I

Defining What Is Me and What Is Not Me

When our children were little, Steve and I lived next door to a family that had children of the same age. I was a relatively new Christian and befriended my neighbor, hoping to love her into the Kingdom. One thing that she didn't particularly enjoy about her life was mothering. So, she began to send her children over every day, beginning early in the morning.

Naive and misguided, I thought the loving thing would be to extend hospitality to these children. My children enjoyed their company, and my neighbor certainly enjoyed having them at my home all day. But it didn't take long before I was weary, resentful, and miserable. Shouldn't a Christian give and give? Even this week's Memory Work seems to imply that—though that is certainly a misreading of the verse.

True love sets boundaries. What is not loving is to take what should be another's responsibilities from them. My neighbor's children needed their mother. But instead of seeing the problem I had created, I exacerbated it by pleading with my husband to move. Tender-hearted, Steve didn't set a boundary with me—and we moved. This was an expensive and unnecessary solution to the problem. How much better if, instead of flight, I had faced my neighbor and set boundaries. I could have said, "I love your children, but I need time alone with my own children. From now on I'd like them to come only when we have set up prearranged play dates." Then I would have had to do the hard work of enforcing the boundary by taking the children home when they came uninvited. I actually think my neighbor might have responded positively to this boundary. But I'll never know, because I chose flight. Boundaries define what is me and what is not me. I needed to be the mother to my children and not to hers.

Memory Work

Begin memorizing Romans 12:20.

Scripture Study

1. Write down the commands of Galatians 6:2 and Galatians 6:5.

At first, the above commands seem contradictory. However, it is helpful to know that the word in verse 2, translated "burden" in the NIV, means "an overburden," whereas the word in verse 5, translated "load" in the NIV, means an "everyday" load. A burden, therefore, would occur when there is unusual stress. Normally, fixing your family's supper would be an everyday load. But if you have a death in your family and many relatives are coming, it becomes an "overburden," and people should come alongside to help.

2. List some examples of everyday loads and then some examples of burdens.

3. Why would it be important to draw a boundary when someone asks you to do his everyday load?

4. Read 2 Thessalonians 3:6–10.

   A. What command does Paul give in verse 6?

   B. What example did Paul and those with him set and why? (vv. 7–9)

   C. What rule did they give them when they were with them? (v. 10)

5. How successfully are you carrying your own everyday load?

DAY 2
. . . .
Boundaries with Children

The most common word to set a boundary is simply no. For the tender-hearted, it isn't always easy to stick to our no. In the 1960's, when our boys were toddlers, my husband and I heard Larry Christenson, the author of *The Christian Family*, speak. He told of the rules in one household:

> The children are not to watch television after supper.

> But if they do watch television, they are not to watch scary movies.

> But if they do watch scary movies, they are not to get in bed with Mommy and Daddy.

> But if they do get in bed with Mommy and Daddy, they are not to bring crackers.

And though we laughed, we knew, to a lesser degree, we had exhibited the same kind of poor parenting. When we give into whining, we reinforce whining. When we look the other way during disobedience, we reinforce disobedience. When there are no consequences for disrespect, we reinforce disrespect. One godly older woman saw a young mother struggling to make her toddler stay in time-out. "Make him sit there, honey, and you might just make it through the teenage years."

Memory Work

Continue memorizing Romans 12:20.

Scripture Study

6. What do you learn about Eli's sons from the following passages?

A. 1 Samuel 2:12–17

B. 1 Samuel 2:22–25

7. What did the Lord tell Samuel about Eli and his family? (vv. 27–36) According to 1 Samuel 3:13, what did Eli fail to do?

8. What can you glean about setting and keeping boundaries from the following passages?

A. Proverbs 15:20

B. Proverbs 19:18

C. Proverbs 22:6

D. Proverbs 22:15

E. Proverbs 23:13–14

One principle Steve and I learned early was "Many rules (or boundaries), many infractions." It's much better to carefully think through the boundaries you choose for your children and be sure you are willing to follow through on them, than to do it thoughtlessly and weaken, teaching the child you do not mean what you say.

9. What warning is given to fathers in Ephesians 6:4? How might this apply to boundaries for children?

10. To whom does Solomon counsel his son to say no to and why?

   A. Proverbs 1:10–19

   B. Proverbs 5:1–12

11. Whom might you counsel your children (or the next generation) to say no to? How might you role play?

12. If you are a mother, grandmother, or aunt—what boundaries have you set for the children in your life? Evaluate how you are doing according to the above Scriptures.

DAY 3
. . . .
Two Are Better Than One

In the adult world, we must deal with people who as children were never trained to respect a no. You may have a grown child, a brother, a friend, or someone in the business world who does not respect your no. If you have legitimate scriptural reasons for saying no and want to remain firm, you may need to find some support. It is difficult to stand up against a "bully" alone; two do better than one.

When Kathy Troccoli was a young singer, her manager asked her to sing a suggestive song. He was sure it would be a hit and was adamant that she do it. She went away for a few days to a Catholic retreat center, looking for the strength to set a boundary. In His merciful timing, a Catholic priest was there to counsel her. He not only told her she must say no, he role played with her, telling her to pretend to pick up a phone and call her manager (whom I will call "Tom"). The priest instructed her: "Kathy—I want you to say, and to keep repeating, no matter what he says, 'I cannot sing that song.'"

Kathy pretended to call: "Tom—I cannot sing that song."

The priest raised his voice: "WHAT DO YOU MEAN? AFTER ALL I'VE DONE FOR YOU?"

Immediately Kathy started to cry and weaken, "I know, I know ..."

"NO! NO! NO! KATRINA. JUST SAY, 'I CANNOT SING THAT SONG.'"

"I cannot sing that song."

"THEN YOU ARE FINISHED! YOUR CAREER IS OVER."

Kathy started to cry again.

"BE STRONG, KATRINA. GOD IS WITH YOU. JUST SAY, 'I cannot sing that song.'"

"I cannot sing that song."

Kathy did stick to her no. That manager left her but she has gone on to experience the anointing of God in a powerful ministry of singing and speaking.

How do we decide when it is right to say no? One clear way is if what we are being asked to do is in violation of God's moral law or if it violates what we know is best for our own spiritual, emotional, or physical health.

Memory Work

Add Romans 12:21 to your Memory Work in Romans 12:20.

Scripture Study

13. What were Shadrach, Meshach, and Abednego commanded to do according to Daniel 3:4–6?

14. How did they respond and why, according to Daniel 3:16–18? Do you think it helped that they were together? Why or why not?

15. Can you think of a time recently when you said no to something that was in violation of God's principles? (The request could have come from a person, from Satan,

or from your own evil desires.)

16. How might you get help from the body of Christ when you have to stand up to someone who is not respecting your no?

DAY 4

Physical Boundaries

When I wrote *The Friendships of Women*, I received an avalanche of mail. Many women wrote because they were being smothered by a friend, or, without realizing it, were smothering a friend who had responded by withdrawing and putting a protective distance between them. The woman doing the smothering often failed to see that she, and not her friend, was at fault. The following letter is typical:

> Michelle and I used to be so close—we talked several times a day and did everything together. But then she began to withdraw. One day I walked into Starbucks and saw her at a table with two friends from our Bible study. They were laughing so hard about something. I felt like I'd been stabbed. I left before they could see me and sobbed all the way home. When I called Michelle, asking her to explain, she told me she was sorry she'd hurt me. But she was cool. Now when I call, I just get her answering machine. What's happened? I feel so betrayed, and I'm so miserable without her. How can I get my friend back?

Memory Work

Finish memorizing Romans 12:20–21.

Scripture Study

17. What does Proverbs 25:17 teach?

A failure to accept a friend's boundaries is often a problem of relational idolatry—looking to that person for what only God can be. At first it can be wonderful to be the recipient of so much attention, but, in time, it becomes a burden. That's how Ginny felt in her relationship with Tom. When she first started dating him, he showered her with affection—and they were inseparable. But soon, she began to miss her time alone. She also missed being with her women friends—but when she tried to explain this, he was hurt. "I love you so much—I don't want to spend an evening without you." It wasn't too long before Ginny broke up with Tom.

18. If you are being smothered, you may need physical space—but it is also an act of kindness to explain this clearly to your friend. What does Proverbs 27:5 say?

19. It is far healthier to have a few close friends than just one. It is also healthier to have friends outside of your husband, rather than expecting him to be all things to you. How would you evaluate this aspect of your life?

Another time we may need physical space is when our emotional, spiritual, or physical life is being threatened. David fled from King Saul when Saul demonstrated a pattern of destruction. After he had tried to kill David three times, David forgave him from his heart, but he also fled.

20. What does Proverbs 22:3 teach?

21. What application do you see for yourself from today's lesson?

DAY 5
· ·
Boundaries Are an Act of Love

Loving boundaries are meant to point an individual to God. When a parent disciplines a child, he is looking toward his future, longing for that child to learn to behave in a way that is pleasing to God. When a wife sets boundaries with an abusive husband, she is longing for him to get help, and to be restored to God. When a friend sets boundaries with a smothering friend, she is showing her that she cannot be all things to her—only God can be that. When we set boundaries on ourselves, to reign in out-of-control spending, eating, or television watching—it is because we know, in our hearts, that we have let something come in the place that only God can be.

Memory Work

Review Romans 12:20–21.

Scripture Study

22. Describe the boundary God sets for us in each of the following and explain why it is an act of love.

    A. Proverbs 5:15–23

    B. Proverbs 13:20

    C. 1 Timothy 6:6–10

    D. 1 Timothy 6:17–19

23. What boundaries do you sense the Spirit of God calling you to heed for yourself?

24. What stood out to you from this lesson? What application will you make for your life?

Prayer Time

Break into groups of three or four. Each woman should lift up the need of her heart and allow her sisters to support her with sentence prayers.

Nine

Experiencing His Power

We understand that we cannot save ourselves, but often we think that we can "will" ourselves to live the Christian life. We are like the sailboat going out on a windless day—we may have gotten a good push from shore, but soon we are dead in the water.

How do we experience the wind in our sails so that, truly, we can be the kind of mothers, daughters, sisters, and friends we long to be?

DAY 1

Living in Love with Jesus

When we fall in love with Jesus, when we truly realize who He is and experience His grace, we are walking on cloud nine. He's real! He's personal! Our days are exciting as we sense His presence, His power, and His peace.

But as time passes, we move out of that honeymoon phase. We may take Him for granted, we may be surprised by the fact that life still has pain. We may become disillusioned about the Christian life and lose our zeal for Him. During this time we may still be going to church, even to Bible study, and trying to live clean—but it's not like it was.

Just as many earthly romances fade after the euphoric infatuation time, so it is in our relationship with Jesus. Instead of abandoning ourselves to Him, we slowly start living for ourselves again. The exciting wind that we first experienced dies. We may get out our paddles to move our boats along, but we become exhausted and discouraged. It doesn't seem to be working.

What is the secret to experiencing the wind of the Spirit again?

Memory Work

Memorize Romans 12:21.

Scripture Study

John the Apostle has a vision recorded in Revelation. Part of that vision involves a message from Jesus to seven different churches.

1. Read Revelation 2:1–7.

   A. What church is being addressed?

   B. How is Jesus described in verse 2?

   C. Who do the stars and who do the lampstands represent? (See Revelation 1:20.)

   The description given of Jesus for each church is also a description of what that particular church needs the most in Him. He is sufficient to meet their lack, to fill their flagging sails.

   D. For what seven things does Jesus praise this church, according to verses 2 and 3?

   E. What is wrong with the church at Ephesus? (v. 4)

F. Has this ever been true of you? (You are working hard, you are doing many good things—but your love for Jesus isn't the same as it was once.) Comment.

* G. Jesus tells this church to do three things. What are they? (v. 5)

R_____

R_____

And_____

H. What warnings and encouragements does He give them? (vv. 5–7)

2. If you were to do what Jesus told the church at Ephesus to do to restore your own love for Him—what would it look like? Be as specific as you can.

   A. Remember the height from which you've fallen. Describe what you were like at the height of your love relationship with Jesus.

   B. Repent. Repent means sincerely confessing and then making a U-turn. Confess, here. And then describe what a true U-turn would look like in your life.

   C. Do the things you did at first. What were some of the things that you did when your love for Jesus was fresh and strong?

DAY 2

Stay the Course

I am blessed to spend time each summer at the lake. My children take me out on a little sunfish sailboat. When the wind first catches the sail, it's exciting, and we whoop, "Oh—here we go!" And then, as the sail billows out with more wind, the speed increases. As we move deeper out into the lake, where the wind is even stronger, we are truly whipping along, needing to lean way back to balance the enormous force that has taken over our sail. However, if we don't cooperate with the wind, if we try to change course, going where we want to go instead of where it is taking us, suddenly, our sail drops, and we lose all our momentum.

One of the most exciting truths in Scripture is that as we stay the course, as we stay in step with the Spirit, choosing the light, choosing to love, our light and our love actually increase. Our speed picks up and, truly, we are experiencing the fullness of His power.

Memory Work

Complete Romans 12:21.

Scripture Study

John's letters are written to believers who wish to experience more of God—more of His power. In his letter he tells us how to become complete and confident in Him.

3. In the following passages, what is the exhortation and what is the promise?

A. 1 John 2:5
   Exhortation

   Promise

B. 1 John 2:28
   Exhortation

Promise

C. 1 John 3:18–20
   Exhortation

Promise

D. 1 John 4:12
   Exhortation

Promise

E. 1 John 4:16–17
   Exhortation

Promise

4. Describe your daily life if you are to "stay the course" and experience more confidence and more completion in the Lord.

DAY 3

Controlled by the Spirit

We are either going to be controlled by our flesh or controlled by the Spirit. Frankly, it's dozens of battles every day. The battle continues throughout our lives, but it is true that as we get in the habit of choosing the light, we develop a "holy groove" that may diminish the battle on some fronts. We may not struggle any more to get out of bed and have our time with God, or we may not struggle to resist overeating. We've experienced the joy of holiness, and it's harder for the Enemy to convince us to change our course. (But he'll still try!) It's helpful to establish holy habits, but we can never stop being diligent. If the Enemy has failed to get us off course in one area, then he'll try another. But we can, through Christ, overcome evil with good.

One of the clearest passages on this is in Romans.

5. Read Romans 7:14–25.

A. Describe Paul's battle with his flesh. (vv. 18–24)

B. Who can give us the victory? (v. 25)

6. Describe the contrast in Romans 8:5.

Pastor Ed House shared with his congregation that the previous week, he had been having an imaginary conversation with someone in his church with whom he had been at odds—and he was carrying on this imaginary conversation on his treadmill. "And I was winning the argument when the Spirit suddenly interrupted and told me to stop!" Pastor House told the Lord he would stop in a minute—he just needed to finish his conversation. But the Spirit told him he didn't need to finish the Devil's business (Door of Life, Rowley's Bay, Wisconsin, August, 2006).

7. Why should we say no to the flesh, according to Romans 8:12?

8. Why should we say yes to the Spirit, according to Romans 8:13–14?

9. How might you say yes to the Spirit in the next few hours?

DAY 4
Out of the Overflow of the Heart, the Mouth Speaks

This summer my son took my eight-year-old grandson charter fishing in Lake Michigan. As the sun rose, sending warm crimson rays over the water, they cast their lines at the place the seasoned fisherman running the boat told them to. Immediately, the action began. Lines were pulled taut, fish came flopping into the boat, and the excitement didn't stop for three hours. When Simeon came back to the cottage, he was starry-eyed. He opened the cooler to reveal twenty-two huge salmon and bass. During the next month, nearly every word out of Simeon's mouth was about fishing.

"Grandma, do you want to go to the hardware store and look at lures?"

"Grandma, did you know that one fish was twenty pounds?"

"Grandma, do you think the fish might be biting now?"

"Grandma, would you be able to take a fish off a hook?"

Jesus said that "out of the overflow of our mouths, the heart speaks." Whatever has a hold on our hearts is going to bubble out, affecting our speech, affecting our actions, affecting our relationships. If what we cherish in our hearts is sweet, then that sweet water spills out to others. But if what we cherish is bitter or worthless, then that unhealthy water spills out, polluting our words and our relationships.

Memory Work

Review Romans 12:9–21.

Scripture Study

10. Read Proverbs 4:23. What does the Lord tell us to do, and why? What images does this proverb bring to mind?

11. What is one way to guard our hearts, according to Psalm 119:11?

12. As you consider the Romans 12 passage you have memorized, can you think of how any part of it has actually affected your actions, has kept you from sinning, or has changed your thought life in the last few months?

13. Christian fellowship can strengthen us to walk in the Spirit—and some believers are more encouraging than others to be around. Often you can tell what is in their hearts by what flows out of their mouths. What believers in your life are particularly encouraging and how might you be around them more?

14. Evaluate what you put into your heart. Consider the following habits that have strengthened Christians enormously down through the ages. If you have adopted

any of these, share what you have done. If you haven't, how might you incorporate it into your life?

A. Listening to Christian radio or taped sermons/music

B. Reading edifying books

C. Praying through the psalms

* 15. Spend fifteen minutes reviewing this guide. Write down the top three lessons you want to remember.

DAY 5
. . . .
Meditating Day and Night

Psalm 1 tells us that the godly meditate on His Word day and night—and they are like trees planted by the water who bring forth fruit season after season. Our vertical relationship has a huge impact on the healthy fruit we hope for in our horizontal relationships. One good Web site on Bible study methods is from Kay Arthur's Precepts Ministry: http://www.preceptaustin.org/a_primer_on_meditation.htm.

Memory Work

We'll close this study with your meditations on Romans 12:9–21.

Scripture Study

16. Write Romans 12:9–21 verse by verse. After each verse, write down, first, your observations. Look carefully at the verse and ask questions such as who, what, why, where, when—ask any question that comes into your mind (a question is a kind of observation). Second, write the verse in your own words, capturing its central meaning. Finally, write down an application to your life.

    A. Romans 12:9

        Observations

        Paraphrase, capturing central meaning

        Application

    B. Romans 12:10

        Observations

        Paraphrase, capturing central meaning

        Application

C. Romans 12:11
   Observations

Paraphrase, capturing central meaning

Application

D. Romans 12:12
   Observations

Paraphrase, capturing central meaning

Application

E. Romans 12:13
   Observations

Paraphrase, capturing central meaning

Application

F. Romans 12:14
   Observations

Paraphrase, capturing central meaning

Application

G. Romans 12:15
   Observations

Paraphrase, capturing central meaning

Application

H. Romans 12:16
    Observations

Paraphrase, capturing central meaning

Application

I. Romans 12:17
    Observations

Paraphrase, capturing central meaning

Application

J. Romans 12:18
    Observations

Paraphrase, capturing central meaning

Application

K. Romans 12:19
   Observations

Paraphrase, capturing central meaning

Application

L. Romans 12:20
   Observations

Paraphrase, capturing central meaning

Application

M. Romans 12:21
   Observations

Paraphrase, capturing central meaning

Application

Memory Verses

Romans 12:9–21

Love must be sincere. Hate what is evil; cling to what is good. Be devoted to one another in brotherly love. Honor one another above yourselves. Never be lacking in zeal, but keep your spiritual fervor, serving the Lord. Be joyful in hope, patient in affliction, faithful in prayer. Share with God's people who are in need. Practice hospitality.

Bless those who persecute you; bless and do not curse. Rejoice with those who rejoice; mourn with those who mourn. Live in harmony with one another. Do not be proud, but be willing to associate with people of low position. Do not be conceited.

Do not repay anyone evil for evil. Be careful to do what is right in the eyes of everybody. If it is possible, as far as it depends on you, live at peace with everyone. Do not take revenge, my friends, but leave room for God's wrath, for it is written: "It is mine to avenge; I will repay," says the Lord. On the contrary:

"If your enemy is hungry, feed him;

if he is thirsty, give him something to drink.

In doing this, you will heap burning coals on his head."

Do not be overcome by evil, but overcome evil with good.

Leader's Helps

For A Woman of Healthy Relationships

ONE
....
The Vertical Relationship

This lesson may need to be divided, especially if the participants have not gotten their guides ahead of time. In that case, go as far as you can and assign the rest of the lesson for the next week.

5. B. Often verses 8–9 are quoted without 10. We are saved by grace—but if salvation is genuine, then His Spirit is in us, equipping us to do the works God had planned for us. As we walk in the Spirit, we are continually being saved from ourselves, we are continually being sanctified.

11. B. See that pattern: As we obey we become more like Jesus.

16. A. His promises and His Word are supernatural sources to help us overcome the sorrow and hatred in this world.

16. B. God can supernaturally protect us from the evil one who is trying to get us to do something that will make God look bad.

Prayer Time

If you have several women who may be new to conversational prayer, demonstrate this first with a few women who are comfortable praying in this manner.

TWO
. . . .
Never Underestimate the Power of a Mother

4. G. We are appointed once (not twice or thrice) to die. One life. Babies don't get to "come back."

THREE
. . . .
Breaking the Chain in Christ

1. E. Husbands are called to protect their wives—and though Abram was in a difficult position, he surely must have known giving Sarai complete free reign could be hard on Hagar. It must have seemed easier for him to wash his hands of Hagar and give in to Sarai, yet it wasn't the merciful way.

8. C. Acknowledging the sins of our fathers helps us to see them and be more likely to not perpetuate them—and calls upon the power of God to help us to do that.

FOUR
Mentoring Children

5. The Greek word for hospitality comes from the Greek words meaning "fond of" and "guests or strangers." Practice indicates a habit—get into the habit of being a lover of guests, particularly those in need, as are strangers. Be a lover of children and of having them in your home.

FIVE
Honoring Family Bonds

2. C. The oil had a sweet fragrance, as harmony is fragrant to God. The oil rolled down—as family harmony rolls down, affecting the next generation. The oil was sacred, used for anointing, as family harmony is sacred to God.

2. E. Dew comes down from higher places, rolling from one mountain to lower mountains. It refreshes and turns the grass and plants green and vibrant.

7. E. Ham was disrespectful of his father and lacking in grace toward him in his vulnerability. Even when our parents fail, we are to honor them and show them courtesy.

SIX
• •
Overcoming Adult Sibling Rivalry

12. D. What Jacob doesn't understand is that we don't control the terms of God's covenant. We are not in the driver's seat. We must come to Him simply because He is God, not in order to get Him to do something for us. Does God ever show mercy toward bargainers? He is often slow to anger and abounding in mercy—but it is the height of presumption to talk this way to God Almighty. Of course, God has the last word, for He is the Potter and we are the clay. He is about to put Jacob over the fire.

SEVEN
• •
Hope for Fractured Families

4. Instead of longing for her husband's love, she simply praises God. Perhaps she is beginning to understand that He is the One who will love her well and never forsake her.

EIGHT
• •
Boundaries for Health

In the area of disciplining children, your group may get into a discussion on spanking, which can be controversial and emotional. Some helpful books on that subject are *Dare to Discipline* (Dobson) and *Boundaries for Kids* (Cloud and Townsend.) There are other ways to discipline, but spanking is scriptural and often can be kinder than methods that are drawn out over time. There is a right way to spank (with regret, calmly) and a wrong way to spank (with anger)—and the child senses the difference. It is also beneficial if the discipline can fit the disobedience—losing privileges for abusing them; writing essays on the importance of being respectful; or doing something kind for someone to whom they have been unkind.

NINE
• •
Experiencing His Power

1. G. Remember the height from which you've fallen.

   Repent.

   Do the things you did at first.

15. Take time with this question.